THE FREDDIE STORIES

LYNDA BARRY

SASQUATCH BOOKS
SEATTLE

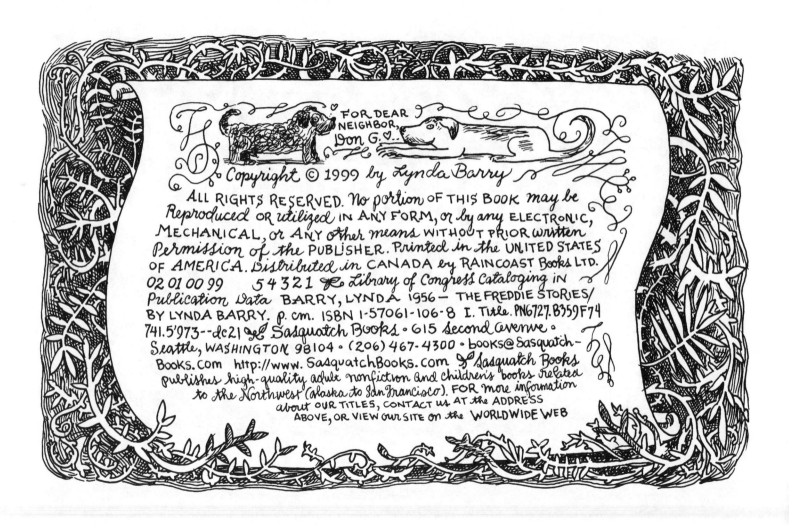

02 01 00 99   5 4 3 2 1   Library of Congress Cataloging in Publication Data BARRY, LYNDA 1956 — THE FREDDIE STORIES/ BY LYNDA BARRY. p. cm. ISBN 1-57061-106-8 I. Title. PN6727.B359F74 741.5'973--dc21   Sasquatch Books • 615 Second Avenue • Seattle, WASHINGTON 98104 • (206) 467-4300 • books@sasquatch-Books.com   http://www.SasquatchBooks.com   Sasquatch Books publishes high-quality adult nonfiction and children's books related to the Northwest (Alaska to San Francisco). FOR more information about OUR TITLES, CONTACT us at the ADDRESS ABOVE, OR VIEW OUR SITE on the WORLDWIDE WEB

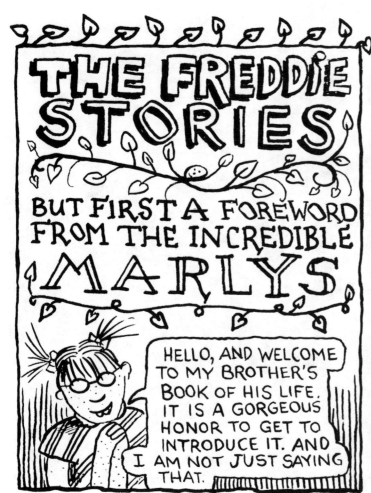

THE FREDDIE STORIES

BUT FIRST A FOREWORD FROM THE INCREDIBLE MARLYS.

HELLO, AND WELCOME TO MY BROTHER'S BOOK OF HIS LIFE. IT IS A GORGEOUS HONOR TO GET TO INTRODUCE IT. AND I AM NOT JUST SAYING THAT.

IT IS NOT A RANK ON MY BROTHER TO SAY HE HAS CERTAIN MENTAL DISORDERS KNOWN AS EMOTIONAL PROBLEMS AND HE IS OFTEN CALLED A FAG AND HAS HAD TO RUN FOR HIS LIFE ON MANY OCCASIONS. HE IS A GENTLE PERSON AND THIS IS A JUVENILE DELINQUENCY WORLD. HE IS SAGITTARIUS AND SOMETIMES QUITE A FREAKSTER.

WHAT'S HAPPENIN'?

WHAT IT IS, MAN.

WHERE IT'S AT.

SAY HEY.

GET DOWN WITH IT.

SOUL FINGER.

NIGHT TRAIN.

JUMP BACK AND KISS YOURSELF.

PSYCHOLOGICAL.

SOMETIMES HIS LIFE HAS BEEN VERY SERIOUSLY TERRIBLE. FOR EXAMPLE HE IS NOT OUR MOM'S FAVORITE PERSON. SHE HAS TOLD HIM MANY TIMES THAT HE WAS NOT SUPPOSED TO HAPPEN. SHE HAS BEEN SCREAMINGLY FRUSTRATED AT HIM FREQUENTLY FOR HIS OWN NATURAL PERSONALITY. AND WE HAVE MOVED A LOT. NEW SCHOOLS BRING TROUBLE. ONE TIME THREE IN ONE YEAR.

MOM? UM,

DON'T SAY "UM."

UH,

DON'T SAY "UH."

WELL, THERE IS A SPIDER—

DON'T TALK TO ME ABOUT INSECTS.

BUT—

NO BUTS.

SO MAYBE A PERSON MIGHT BE WONDERING, WILL FREDDIE GET HIS HAPPY ENDING? WILL THE EMOTIONALLY DISTURBED FAG FINALLY WALK FREE THROUGH THE DAISIES OF HAPPINESS? AND WHAT WILL HE HAVE TO DO TO GET THERE?

WOW. OK.

DAG.

THANK YOU, MARLYS, FOR THAT MAGNETIC INTRODUCTION.

IMPH NOTPH PHINISHPH!

MPHREDDIEPH!

SO, LIKE, UM, UH.... UH, UM, TURN THE PAGE WHENEVER YOU WANT, OK?

COOKING with FREDDIE!

SAY YOUR SISTERS ARE HUNGRY AND YOU WANT TO FIX THEM DINNER. HERE'S A THING: FRIED BALONEY SANDWICH! BREAD = CARBOHYDRATE. PUT ON SOME LETTUCE = VEGETABLE. THE MEAT IS THE BALONEY. DRINK IT DOWN WITH MILK. ADD IT TOGETHER. IT EQUALS <u>FOUR</u> FOOD GROUPS!

you will need...

1. BREAD
2. FRYING PAN
3. STACK OF BALONEY
4. TURNER THING
5. MAYONNAISE
6. A CHAIR TO STAND ON
7. STOVE

1. DRAG YOUR CHAIR TO THE STOVE AND STICK ON THE FRYING PAN. LIGHT UP THE STOVE. PEEL OPEN THE BALONEY PACKAGE. PEEL OFF A BALONEY. DROP IT ONTO THE FRYING PAN. IF YOUR SISTER TELLS YOU IT'S A WASTE OF TIME BECAUSE SHE IS NOT GOING TO LIKE IT, SHE IS <u>WRONG</u>.

I WILL NOT LIKE IT.

YOU ARE WRONG.

2. KEEP YOUR EYES ON THE BALONEY AND WAIT FOR THE MAGIC. YOU WILL SEE IT! THE BALONEY WILL GO IN A HUMP. IT WILL POP UP IN SLOW MOTION. TURN IT OVER AND IT WILL MAGICALLY HUMP AGAIN! FRIED BALONEY IS VERY GOOD A LITTLE BURNT. BURNT ON THE EDGES IS GREAT. THEN PUT MAYONNAISE ON THE BREAD, PUT THE BALONEY AND LETTUCE, AND THE SMELL WILL BE ALLURING.

← (SHE IS FLOATING ON THE ODOR)

MMM!

I WAS SPAZZING OUT WHEN I SAID I DID NOT WANT SOME!

COME AND GET IT!

(THE TEENAGER IS SO INTERESTED)

3. WHAT IS REALLY GOOD IS IF YOU ALSO HAVE POTATO CHIPS TO PUT IN THE SANDWICH AND A BANANA TO EAT WITH IT. AND A GIANT MILK AND WHAT IS REALLY GOOD IS IF YOU EAT ON TV TRAYS IN FRONT OF YOUR FAVORITE SHOW. TRY IT ON YOUR SISTERS OR ANYONE WHO IS HUNGRY AND SAD. IT IS THE BEST FOOD FOR SAD PEOPLE! THAT'S ALL FOLKS UNTIL NEXT TIME FROM YOUR WORLD-FAMOUS CHEF OF COOKING, I'M FREDDIE.

FREDDIE, YOU ARE INCREDIBLE AND THIS SANDWICH IS ALSO VERY INCREDIBLE

THIS SANDWICH IS WICKED.

WHAT IS GREAT ABOUT SUMMER

IN SUMMER I LOVE ALL THE INSECTS. THIS SUMMER I AM LOOKING FORWARD TO MOSTLY INSECTS. WHAT ARE MY FAVORITES? I ADMIRE FLIES. ESPECIALLY THIS ONE FLY. IT USED TO LIVE IN MY ROOM. BEFORE I CAME TO MY COUSIN'S HOUSE. MY MOM TRIED TO KILL IT BUT IT ALWAYS ESCAPED. SHE SAID THAT IT CAN'T BE THE SAME FLY. BUT IT WAS. IT WAS THE FLY CALLED JEFF.

HE HAS SAT ON MY FINGER. I HAVE LOOKED IN HIS EYES. CALLED COMPOUND EYES. WHEN HE LOOKS AT ME HE SEES AROUND 300 OF MY HEADS. AND HE BREATHES THROUGH HOLES ON HIS ABDOMEN. IF YOU LOOK CLOSE YOU CAN SEE THE MOVEMENT OF IT. HIS HEARING MEMBRANE IS ON THE SIDE OF HIS ABDOMEN. I HAVE WHISPERED TO JEFF. I SANG HIM THE SONG "FOOL ON THE HILL." I TRIED TO GET JEFF TO RIDE AROUND ON THE RECORD PLAYER BUT FLIES WON'T.

ONCE HE GOT STUCK IN THE LIGHT FIXTURE BUT I GOT HIM OUT BY PUTTING A CHAIR ON A CHAIR ON MY BED. I UNSCREWED THE LIGHT FIXTURE AND FOUND THE FLY GRAVEYARD. IT WAS ABOUT 17 DEAD FLIES BUT TO JEFF IT LOOKED LIKE AROUND 2,400.
IF MY MOM DIDN'T YELL I WOULD HAVE NEVER DROPPED THE LIGHT FIXTURE.

JEFF! JEFF! SPEAK TO ME!

HOLY MOTHER OF GOD!

WHY I LOVE SUMMER IS BECAUSE IT'S WARM AND SUNNY OUTSIDE. WHY I THINK SUMMER IS GREAT IS YOU CAN OPEN YOUR WINDOWS AND FINALLY JEFF IS FREE, FINALLY THE FLY-SWATTER IS GONE FROM HIS LIFE. SO IF YOU ARE WALKING BY A GARBAGE CAN IN THE ALLEY AND YOU SEE A FLY, SAY "RIGHT ON" TO IT FOR ME IN CASE IT IS JEFF. SAY HI FROM YOUR OLD PAL FREDDIE.

SO LONG, MY FRIEND.

I WILL ALWAYS MISS YOU.

INTRODUCING THE PEOPLE: Starting with Cousin Arnold

MY COUSIN KEEPS A DIARY. HE WROTE,"LOOK AT THAT TREE, LOOK AT THAT TREE, I THINK THAT I SHALL NEVER SEE A POEM AS LOVELY AS... ALL MY LIFE PEOPLE BEEN SAYING THAT, AND FOR WHAT? BECAUSE I LOOKED AT THE TREE AND DIDN'T SEE NOTHING.

MAYBE A SQUIRREL RUNNING IN THE TOP BRANCH AND WITH MY DAISY RIFLE I WILL SHOOT HIS LITTLE ASS. FROM MY WINDOW UP HERE I HAVE SHOT MANY LITTLE ASSES WITH MY DAISY. SHOT THEM OUT OF THAT TREE AND I HAVE EVEN SHOT THE TREE ITSELF ON SLOW DAYS. TODAY IS A SLOW DAY AND THAT TREE IS DYING.

I HAVE WHAT IS CALLED A VERY BORED LIFE AND NOW IT IS SUMMER AND MY COUSIN FREDDIE IS A FAG. AND THAT TREE IS BLOCKING MY VIEW OF THE CORNER. OF THE ACTION OF WHICH THERE IS NONE. IN MY SITUATION PEOPLE SET THINGS ON FIRE. I HAVE A FRIEND NAME OF JIM-JIMMY-JIM. OH MY GOSH HOW HE HATES FAGS.

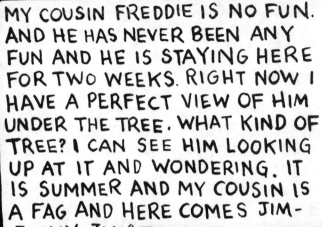

MY COUSIN FREDDIE IS NO FUN. AND HE HAS NEVER BEEN ANY FUN AND HE IS STAYING HERE FOR TWO WEEKS. RIGHT NOW I HAVE A PERFECT VIEW OF HIM UNDER THE TREE. WHAT KIND OF TREE? I CAN SEE HIM LOOKING UP AT IT AND WONDERING. IT IS SUMMER AND MY COUSIN IS A FAG AND HERE COMES JIM-JIMMY-JIM."

I KNOW WHO YOU ARE.

NEVER BEEN

WE HAD TO GO VISIT MY UNCLE IN THE NUT HOUSE AND HE TOLD ABOUT BEING A BUM IN POCATELLO, IDAHO AND GETTING HIT ON THE HEAD BY A UNION PACIFIC RAILROAD MAN AND IN JACKSONVILLE, FLORIDA THEY ALSO BASHED HIS HEAD IN. A SEABOARD COASTLINE RAILROAD MAN DID IT.

BUT IN MINOT, NORTH DAKOTA THE RAILROAD MEN TREAT YOU RIGHT AND ALSO IN CLEVELAND, OHIO THEY TREAT YOU GOOD, GOOD VERY GOOD INDEED, THAT'S THE CONRAIL LINE. AND THEY AREN'T HALF BAD IN MILWAUKEE, BUT STAY AWAY FROM LINCOLN, NEBRASKA. THEM BURLINGTON NORTHERN MEN COME AT YOU WITH TIRE IRONS.

BULLS IS THE NAME OF THE RAIL-ROAD POLICE. CHRIST, THEY DON'T GOT NO HEARTS AT ALL IN TYLER, TEXAS, THAT'S THE COTTON BELT LINE. AND YOU'D RATHER BE DEAD THAN IN THE YARDS IN MINNEAPOLIS, THAT DAMN BURLINGTON NORTHERN, YOU'D BE BETTER OFF AVOIDING BUR-LINGTON NORTHERN ALTOGETHER, COLD-HEARTED BASTARDS, THEY CALL THEIR CLUBS `PERSUADERS' AND THEY USE THEM EVEN ON THE GRANDPAS. SEEN IT. SEEN MEN DIE.

YEAH, YEAH.

TIME TO GO.

IN THE CAR ON THE WAY HOME MY AUNT DRIVES ALONG THE RAILROAD TRACKS AND A TRAIN ROLLS BY WITH A HEADLIGHT BRIGHT IN THE MIDDLE OF THE DAY. ON THE CARS I READ B·U·R·L·I·N·G·T·O·N N·O·R·T·H·E·R·N. I SAY TO MY AUNT, "I DIDN'T KNOW UNCLE BOYD WAS A HOBO." THE TRAIN BLOWS THE WHISTLE AND MY AUNT SNORTS OUT CIGARETTE SMOKE. "BOYD?" SHE SAYS, "BOYD'S NEVER BEEN ON A TRAIN IN HIS LIFE."

11

THE Very PINK Flowers

THAT FRIEND OF MY COUSIN ARNOLD.
THAT KID NAMED JIM-JIMMY-JIM. HE
IS A FIRE LOVER. THE LOVER OF
LIGHTER FLUID AND CHARCOAL WIZARD.
JIM-JIMMY-JIM. WHEN HIS MOTHER
CALLS HIM, HE RUNS THE OTHER WAY
AND MY COUSIN, HE FOLLOWS.

AND I WILL ADMIT I FOLLOWED THEM
AS A SPY AND JIM-JIMMY-JIM SAYS
HIS SISTER IS AN IDIOT AND THAT IS
WHY HE HAS TO BURN HER NIGHT-
GOWN BEHIND THE SCHOOL. HE HAD
IT IN A PAPER BAG. A COP CAR CAME
BY AND I SAW THEM CHANGE POS-
TURES AND TRY TO LOOK INNOCENT
BUT THE COP DIDN'T EVEN NOTICE
THEM. JIM-JIMMY-JIM IS MAD THAT
HIS SISTER IS IN LOVE WITH THIS
GUY NAMED HECTOR. A SPEAKER OF
SPANISH. ILLEGAL.

JIM-JIMMY-JIM SAID "HOLD THIS" AND HANDED THE NIGHTGOWN TO ARNOLD. HIS SISTER IS 17. ARNOLD IS SMELLING THE NIGHTGOWN AND JIM-JIMMY-JIM SLUGS HIM. "GIVE IT," SAYS HE. "KNOCK IT OFF." ARNOLD LOOKS DOWN. HER NAME IS JOANNE. LEAVES GET PILED ON THE NIGHTGOWN. PINK FLOWERS IN A PATTERN.

LIGHTER FLUID, LIGHTER FLUID, BACK UP, HERE GOES. JIM-JIMMY-JIM CAN LIGHT A MATCH IN ONE TRY. "BACK UP," HE SAYS, "HERE GOES." FIRE. BRIGHT. FIRE. OH. HE STARES AT IT WITH NO BLINKS. "HEY!" SOME ONE SHOUTS, "HEY! HEY!" ARNOLD TAKES OFF RUNNING. JIM-JIMMY-JIM JUST STANDS THERE. THE PINK FLOWERS OF JOANNE BURN AND BURN IN MY BRAIN. THEY ARE BURNING NOW. RIGHT NOW. "HEY!" I SHOUTED AGAIN. JIM-JIMMY-JIM DIDN'T EVEN TURN HIS HEAD.

MY·DISCOVERY

THE REASON IS JOANNE. WHY ARNOLD FOLLOWS JIM-JIMMY-JIM ON HIS INSANE MISSIONS. ARNOLD IS IN LOVE WITH HER. WITH HER WHO IS 17 AND SNEAKING OUT AT NIGHT TO SEE THE FORBIDDEN HECTOR WHO SPEAKS SPANISH TO HER, WHO SINGS IT, SOY DEL BARRIO DEL ALTO.

HE DANCES TO THESE CERTAIN WORDS AND UNDER THE STREET-LIGHT HIS REFLECTION IS IN HER EYES. ARNOLD AND JIM-JIMMY-JIM WATCH FROM THE BUSHES AND I WATCH THEM. JIM-JIMMY-JIM HAS A MILK BOTTLE AND IN THE MILK BOTTLE IS GASOLINE.

DROP BY DROP HE HAS COLLECTED IT FROM THE NOZZLE AT MITCHELL'S GAS STATION. "ALMOST GOT ENOUGH," HE WHISPERS. HECTOR TAKES THE BEAUTIFUL JOANNE IN HIS ARMS AND ARNOLD STARES. "ALMOST GOT ENOUGH TO BURN HIS HOUSE DOWN." THERE IS KISSING. "JOANNE, JOANNE," IN A SPANISH ACCENT. INTO THE DARKNESS THEY VANISH.

IN HER YARD ARNOLD WAITS NEXT TO JIM-JIMMY-JIM. IN THE SHADOW OF THE GARAGE THEY WAIT FOR THE RETURN OF JOANNE, TO WATCH HER CLIMB THE TREE TO HER OPEN WINDOW, THEY WAIT AND WAIT BUT THE ONLY PERSON WHO IS STILL AWAKE TO SEE HER DO IT IS ME.

HECTOR

SO MUSIC IS COMING OUT OF HECTOR'S HOUSE, IT'S WARM AND THE WINDOWS ARE OPEN AND ARNOLD AND JIM-JIMMY-JIM ARE SPYING FROM THEIR USUAL SPOT AND I AM SPYING FROM MINE. THEY ARE WATCHING AN OLD LADY WITH BRAIDS BRING HECTOR FOOD.

IN THE YELLOW-LIT WINDOW, HECTOR AND THE GRANDMA ARE LAUGHING. JIM-JIMMY-JIM SOCKS ARNOLD, SAYS, "KEEP YOUR HEAD DOWN." AND THAT HE HAS ENOUGH NOW, ENOUGH GASOLINE. JIM-JIMMY-JIM CHECKS HIS MATCHES.

TONIGHT IS JUST PRACTICE. TO-NIGHT IS PRACTICE FOR THE RE-VENGE, FOR WHEN JIM-JIMMY-JIM PAYS HECTOR BACK FOR TOUCHING THE BEAUTIFUL JOANNE. "HECTOR," HE WHISPERS AND LIGHTS A MATCH. "HECTOR, HECTOR." THE LIGHTS GO OFF. THE HOUSE IS DARK. "WHAT TIME?" HE SAYS. "11:57," SAYS ARNOLD. JIM-JIMMY-JIM WRITES IT IN A RED NOTEBOOK. HE HAS BEEN WATCHING MANY DAYS.

"LET'S GO," SAYS HE. BUT FROM UP THE STREET COMES SOMEONE WALKING FAST. THE SOUND OF GIRL FEET MOVING TOWARD THE HOUSE. "HECTOR, HECTOR," SHE WHISPERS. "I WILL KILL HIM," SAYS JIM-JIMMY-JIM. "JOANNE," ARNOLD WHISPERS. AND THEN HECTOR'S FRONT DOOR OPENS. JOANNE GOES INSIDE. "TOMORROW," SAYS JIM-JIMMY-JIM. "TOMORROW."

AFTER MIDNIGHT

WHEN YOU ARE THE FRIEND OF A VERY MEAN PERSON YOU FEEL CERTAIN THEY WOULD NEVER DO TO YOU WHAT THEY CONSTANTLY DO TO OTHER PEOPLE. IT'S NOT LOGICAL BUT YOU STILL THINK IT. UNTIL YOU MAKE THEM MAD.

YOU SLEEP AT MY HOUSE TOMORROW. TELL YOUR MOM.

OK. YEAH. SEE YA.

I'LL COME GET YOU AFTER DINNER.

OK. SEE YA. BYE.

MEAN PERSONS CAN BE THRILLING WHEN THEY ARE YOUR GOOD FRIEND. THEY WILL DO THE THINGS BOLD AND DANGEROUS AND SO COLD-BLOODED AND IT WILL BE NERVOUSLY EXCITING TO WITNESS AND YOU WILL FEEL BIG, EVEN HUGE. THEY DEMAND LOYALTY AND YOU DEMAND NOTHING EXCEPT TAKE-ME-ALONG.

I'M A IDIOT - I'M A IDIOT - I'M A IDIOT. I AM SO STUPID. I AM SO SCREWED.

THEY TAKE YOU TO SEE THE FUTURE. TOMORROW THAT HOUSE WILL BE BLACK AND SMOKING. TOMORROW EVERYONE WILL BE SAYING WHO DID IT, WHO DID IT. YOU DID IT, SAID JIM-JIMMY-JIM, IT'S YOU WHO'S GOING TO LIGHT IT. "WHAT?" SAID MY COUSIN. "IT'S A TEST," SAID JIM-JIMMY-JIM, "A TEST OF HOW TRUE YOU ARE."
ARNOLD, ARNOLD, PSSST, ARNOLD.
WHA-
I'LL BOOST YOU. WANT A BOOST UP INTO THE WINDOW?
YOU BEEN FOLLOWING ME? YOU WANNA GET KILLED?
"ARE YOU TRUE?" JIM-JIMMY-JIM LIT A MATCH. "SWEAR YOU'RE TRUE?" ARNOLD NODDED. "IF YOU'RE TRUE YOU WON'T FLINCH." JIM-JIMMY-JIM PUSHED THE LIT MATCH INTO MY COUSIN'S BARE ARM. "OW! OW! OW!" HE JERKED AWAY. JIM-JIMMY-JIM SAID, "FAG."
YOU A SPY? KNOW WHAT HAPPENS TO SPIES?
WHICH KIND?
YOUR KIND.
OH, LIKE 007?

The Morning

EXCUSE ME, EXCUSE ME, YOUR NAME IS HECTOR, RIGHT? – HE LOOKS AT ME -- YOU'RE THE BOY-FRIEND OF JOANNE, RIGHT? – HE REALLY LOOKS AT ME. WE'RE AT THE BUS STOP. HE'S GOING TO WORK. JANITOR. BAKER HOS-PITAL. THE STITCHED NAME ON HIS UNIFORM POCKET SAYS "NICK."

EXCUSE ME, IT'S IMPORTANT. AND I TELL HIM. ALL OF IT. EVERYTHING. TONIGHT, I SAY. "THIS NIGHT?" HE SAYS. YES. YES. YOU SHOULD CALL THE POLICE. "NO POLICE." HE WAVES HIS HANDS. "NO POLICE." WHEN HIS BUS COMES, HE SHAKES MY HAND AND SAYS IT AGAIN. "NO POLICE."

WHAT WERE YOU DOING UP SO EARLY?

WENT FOR A WALK.

LORD GOD, MY HEAD HURTS. I'M GETTING OLD. 3 BEERS IS MY LIMIT.

AT DINNERTIME THE LONG SHADOW OF JIM-JIMMY-JIM CROSSES THE PORCH. MY AUNT YELLS, "WE'RE STILL EATING!" THE SHADOW SAYS, "I'LL WAIT." THE PLAN WAS A SLEEPOVER BUT ARNOLD DIDN'T WANT TO GO. IN A SOFT VOICE HE SAID, "I'M SICK, MOM. MY STOMACH, MOM. TELL HIM, MOM. HOW YOU'RE MAKING ME STAY HOME TONIGHT." MY AUNT SQUINTED.

WHAT SICK?

UM. YOU SAID YOU COULD ONLY DRINK 3 BEERS BUT NOW YOU'RE ON NUMBER FIVE.

I NEVER SAID THAT.

"SICK?!" SHE SAID. "WHAT KIND OF BALONEY IS THIS? SICK? YOU'RE UP TO SOMETHING." HER VOICE WAS VERY LOUD. "GO TELL HIM YOURSELF. I'M NOT LYING FOR YOU." ARNOLD STOOD UP. "I'M ABOUT TO BARF." I SAID, "IT'S OK. I'LL TELL HIM," AND I WENT TO THE SCREEN DOOR. I LOOKED LEFT AND I LOOKED RIGHT. THE SHADOW WAS GONE.

GONE?

YUH-HUH

I THINK I MIGHT BE DEAD

I THINK I POSSIBLY JUST DIED.

RED SPARKS FLY

I HEAR FIRE TRUCKS. DID HE DO IT? IS HECTOR'S HOUSE ON FIRE? I HEAR SIRENS SCREAMING IN THAT DIRECTION. MY COUSIN SAYS, "WHAT ARE YOU DOING? FREDDIE! FREDDIE!" I CLIMB OUT THE BEDROOM WINDOW AND RUN ACROSS THE DARK YARD.

THE STARS ARE BRIGHT AND POWERFUL THROUGH THE BERZERK BLACK BRANCHES OF TREES. I'M RUNNING TO WHERE THE RED SPARKS ARE FLYING. TO THE CHOKING SMOKE. AND I WAS CONCENTRATING ON THAT. THEN BLAM! I GET BASHED ON THE HEAD AND EVERYTHING GOES WHITE. JIM-JIMMY-JIM IS THERE SCREAMING HE KNOWS IT WAS ME. KICKING HARD SHOES INTO MY SIDE AND SAYING I MUST DIE FOR MY CRIME OF WARNING HECTOR.

CRACK

AFTER THAT, I DON'T KNOW. THE SMELL OF SMOKE, THE SMELL OF BURNING AND THEN FILL-IN-THE BLANK. IT WAS 16 STITCHES ON THE BACK OF MY HEAD. THE HOUSE THAT BURNED DOWN WASN'T HECTOR'S. HIM AND HIS FRIENDS WERE WAITING FOR JIM-JIMMY-JIM IN A CIRCLE SO JIM-JIMMY-JIM BURNED A DIFFERENT HOUSE INSTEAD.

AND THE HOUSE HAD A LADY IN IT AND THAT LADY DIED. AND THE POLICE CAME KNOCKING AND ASKING FOR MY COUSIN BECAUSE JIM-JIMMY-JIM TOLD THEM ARNOLD PLANNED IT ALL OUT, SAID ARNOLD WAS THE MASTER MIND, HE WAS JUST OBEYING ARNOLD AND INTO THE POLICE CAR WENT ARNOLD AND MY AUNT SAID I WAS NEVER ALLOWED TO COME THERE AGAIN. MY INFLUENCE IS SOMETHING TERRIBLE.

JUVENILE

DO YOU KNOW JUVENILE? THE LOCK-DOWN DESTINATION FOR MY COUSIN, FOR ME TOO NOW THAT JIM-JIMMY-JIM HAS NAMED ME TO THE COPS. ALL THREE OF US, HE SAID, WE PLANNED THE FIRE TOGETHER. THE CALL HAS BEEN MADE TO MY MOM.

HELL **NO** I'M NOT DRIVING 200 MILES TO PICK HIM UP! HE'S GOING TO LEARN HIS LESSON! KEEP HIM THERE!

DO YOU UNDERSTAND THE SERI-OUSNESS? ASKED MR. BOHDY, MY JUVIE OFFICER. A WOMAN LOST HER LIFE BECAUSE OF YOU. WHY DIDN'T YOU TELL THE POLICE? HECTOR IN MY MEMORY WAVED HIS HANDS, SAYING "NO POLICE, NO POLICE." I TOLD MR. BOHDY. HE CALLED ME AN IDIOT.

OH FOR THE LOVE OF GOD. SO THAT LADY DIED BECAUSE YOU WERE PROTECTING SOME DAMN MEXICAN? YOU HOLLOW-HEADED—

BUT I DIDN'T—

DON'T INTERRUPT ME.

BUT I — —

DO **NOT**.

MAYBE I AM WARPED IN THE BRAINS AS MANY PEOPLE ALL MY LIFE HAVE TOLD ME. THERE IS SOMETHING WRONG, SOMETHING WRONG WITH YOU, FREDDIE, SOMETHING WRONG WITH YOU. YOU GOT NO JUDGMENT OF PEOPLE. OF SITUATIONS. NONE. NONE.

HEL-LO DEAD BOY..

JIM-JIMMY-JIM IS IN BUNK 3. ARNOLD IS IN 7. THEY ARE NOT SURE WHERE TO PUT THE RAT. BECAUSE JUVIE IS A DEADLY PLACE FOR RATS LIKE ME. I BELONG TO JIM-JIMMY-JIM. THE STORY IS OUT AND EVERYBODY WANTS TO SEE IT HAPPEN. WHEN JIM-JIMMY-JIM CATCHES ME IN THE CORNER, EVERYONE WANTS TO BE THERE TO SEE.

BLUBBO.

FREDDIE.

YOU THE FAG THAT BUSTED JIM-JIM?

UM. YEAH.

DAG, GUY. WHAT'S IT LIKE BEING DEAD?

What it is like to be Dead.

ONE THING THAT THERE TURNS OUT TO BE WHEN YOU ARE DEAD IS VIOLENCE. VIOLENCE ON EVERY SIDE. BEING DEAD IS SO VIOLENT. THERE ARE VIOLENT DEAD PEOPLE EVERYWHERE. I HAVE FOUND A SCIENCE BOOK AND I AM STARING AT IT HARD. THE CELL MEMBRANE.

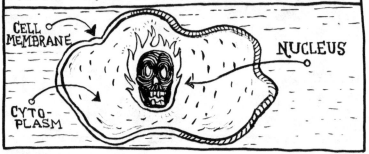

CELL MEMBRANE

NUCLEUS

CYTO-PLASM

THE CELL MEMBRANE CONTROLS THE FLOW OF MATERIALS IN AND OUT OF THE CELL, OUT OF THE BUNK, HE IS IN BUNK 3 AND I AM IN 5 AND HE HAS A CLEAR VIEW OF ME. BLUBBO CHECKS AND HE'S STILL LOOKING, WAITING FOR MY EYES TO LAND ON HIS CELLS HIS EYE CELLS. EVERY LIVING THING IS MADE OF CELLS. THEY ARE THE UNITS OF BEING ALIVE.

3

JAMES, JIM J.

ONLY THINGS MADE OF CELLS BURN AND ONLY THINGS MADE OF CELLS DIE. THE LADY MADE OUT OF CELLS AND THE HOUSE MADE OUT OF CELLS. "HE'S SAYING SOMETHING" SAYS BLUBBO. "HIS LIPS ARE MOVING ON THE SAME WORD." EVERY MINUTE A HUNDRED MILLION CELLS IN YOUR BODY DIE. UNLESS YOU ARE ON FIRE.

HEY FREDDIE!
HEY FREDDIE!
HEY FREDDIE!
HEY FREDDIE!

THEN THE DYING CELLS CANNOT BE COUNTED. "HE'S SAYING YOUR NAME," SAYS BLUBBO, "HE'S SAYING FREDDIE, FREDDIE, FREDDIE." WHAT WAS THE NAME OF THE LADY? NO ONE WILL TELL ME. "HE WANTS YOU," SAYS BLUBBO, "HE WANTS TO SEE YOU." BURNING CHANGES THINGS, A VOICE IN MY BRAIN CELLS SAYS, "BURNING CHANGES EVERYTHING," A LADY'S VOICE, A SCALDED VOICE, HERS.

SHE WAS SHE WASN'T

WHO WAS SHE? JIM-JIMMY-JIM
DON'T CARE A LICK, HE IS NOT
GUILTY, NOWHERE INSIDE OF HIM
FEELING GUILTY. THE WAY IT HAP-
PENED NEVER HAPPENED. IT HAP-
PENED THE WAY HE SAYS IT DID.
IN HIS MIND HE MAKES THE WORLD.
WHO WAS SHE? SHE WASN'T.

NUCLEUS, CYTOPLASM, ENDO-
PLASMIC RETICULUM, SHE WAS
THIS IN THE MORNING BUT THAT
NIGHT SHE CHANGED. WHO WAS
SHE? DON'T ASK, SAID MOM. I
HAVE BEEN RELEASED. THE NOTE-
BOOKS OF JIM-JIMMY-JIM HAD
ALL THE EVIDENCE. MOM HAD TO
DRIVE FIVE HOURS BECAUSE
MY AUNT WOULDN'T TAKE ME.
WHO WAS SHE? WHO WAS SHE?

BYE BLUBBO.

YEAH.

LUCKY DOG.

WANT ME TO WRITE YOU?

I DON'T CARE.

OH...

WHAT ARE YOU STARING AT?

MOM...

DON'T TALK TO ME. JUST GET IN THE CAR. I'M SO MAD AT YOU.

"I DON'T KNOW AND I DON'T CARE," SAID MOM. "WHERE THE HELL'S THE DAMN HIGHWAY? I'M GOING IN CIRCLES." SHE TURNS DOWN ALL THE WRONG STREETS UNTIL IT IS BEFORE US. THE REMAINS OF THE HOUSE WITH POLICE TAPE AROUND IT. ON THE FRONT WALK SITS A CAT. HER CAT?

"LORD GOD," SAYS MOM. "LOOK AT IT. LOOK AT IT GOOD," AND THEN SHE SMACKS MY FACE SO HARD. "YOU SEE WHAT YOU PUT ME THROUGH?" I WONDER DID THE DEAD LADY GUIDE THE CAR THERE. I WONDER IS SHE FURIOUS WITH ME. "I'M SORRY," I SAY AND THE SORRYS COME BAWLING OUT. MOM LOOKS CONTENTED. SHE THINKS THOSE SORRYS ARE HERS.

29

DEAR·BLUBBO,

DEAR BLUBBO, HOW IS IT GOING? IT IS FINE HERE. MY SISTERS ARE FINE. MOM IS USUAL. EVERYTHING IS REGULAR IN LIFE EXCEPT I AM STILL SEEING THE BURNING SKULL HEADS. YESTERDAY MOM TOOK ME TO SEARS FOR SCHOOL CLOTHES.

SALE

BACK TO SCHOOL

MAY I HELP YOU?

YEAH. YOU WANT A KID?

HA-HA. HA-HA.

I'LL GIVE HIM TO YOU CHEAP.

HA-HA.

I TOLD MY SISTERS I COULD SEE THE PEOPLE'S HEAD BONES. THEY SAID **DO NOT** TELL MOM. A GUY MOVED A TRAILER ONTO THE EMPTY LOT BY OUR HOUSE. HIS SKULL IS SPECTACULAR, MANY COLORS GLOWING. I DID NOT GET NEW SHOES BECAUSE MY FEET ARE STILL THE SAME SIZE AS LAST YEAR. ALL OF ME IS.

HOW ABOUT MINE? CAN YOU SEE MINE?

YEAH

IS IT CUTE?

MAR-LYS

SHHH!

IS IT?

IT STARTS NEXT WEEK. MY TEACHER WILL BE MR. FILE WHO IS KNOWN AS A HARD TEACHER WITH MANY RULES. MY SISTER MARLYS HAD HIM. SHE SAYS SHE FEELS VERY SORRY FOR ME. I AM STARTING TO GET USED TO THE SKULL HEADS.

MR. FILE.

THIS IS HIM. HE ALWAYS SMELLS LIKE VAPO RUB.

MR. FILE ROOM 7 MARTIN EDWAY ELEMENTARY

MY VERY WORST TEACHER RIGHT THERE.

WELL BLUBBO, THAT IS ALL I CAN THINK OF. THE HAIR IS GROWING BACK AROUND MY STITCHES AND MY SISTER SAYS IT LOOKS VERY FRANKENSTEIN. I SAID IT COULD BE THE MAN WITH THE X-RAY EYES. I SAID MAYBE WHEN I GOT BASHED IN THE HEAD I GOT THE X-RAY POWERS. POSSIBLY. OR IT IS THE LADY. HAVE YOU EVER HEARD OF A GHOST THAT HAUNTS THE EYE-BALLS? PLEASE WRITE BACK. FROM FREDDIE.

GUY IS PSYCHO.

GUY FREAKS ME.

DENNIS THE BABY

ON THE STREET BY THE FIRE STATION IS WHERE I SAW THEM. THE LADY HAD A SKULL HEAD BUT THE BABY DIDN'T. SHE IS ONLY 17 AND SHE LIVES IN THE CROWN APARTMENTS, 1E. DENNIS THE BABY DOESN'T HAVE TEETH YET. HE SMILED AT ME.

EXCUSE ME BUT YOU GOT AN EXCELLENT BABY.

YOU WANT HIM?

THE LADY'S LIFE IS MOSTLY TV. IN THE DAY, IN THE NIGHT, JUST TV, TV, TV. I WENT THERE, SHE LET ME FEED HIM WHILE SHE SMOKED KOOLS AND RUBBED LOTION ON HER LEGS AND TOLD ME ABOUT THE PEOPLE ON "GENERAL HOSPITAL".

HER! RIGHT THERE. BIGGEST WHORE ON THE SHOW.

THAT'S THE ONE I WAS SAYING. SEE? DOESN'T SHE JUST LOOK IT?

I AM GOOD AT MAKING DEN-
NIS LAUGH AND YOU CAN SEE
WHERE TINY DENTURES WOULD
FIT IF THEY MADE THEM FOR
BABIES. SHE CALLS HIM THE
MENACE. SHE SAID HE CONTROLS
HER LIFE AND SHE IS CLIMBING
THE WALLS AND SHE NEEDS TO
BE WITH THE PEOPLE AND CAN
I BABYSIT AND I SAID YES AND
INSTANTLY SHE WAS GONE.

SLAM!

AND THEN IT GOT DARK AND
SHE DID NOT COME BACK. IT
WAS LATE AND SHE DIDN'T
HAVE A PHONE AND I THOUGHT
MOM WOULD BE FURIOUSLY
WONDERING. I WAS GETTING
NERVOUS AND DENNIS WAS ALSO
VERY NERVOUS. WHEN THE LADY
FINALLY CAME BACK SHE WAS
WOBBLY AND THEN BARFING.
SHE BEGGED ME DON'T GO. PLEASE.
"THINK OF DENNIS", SHE SAID.
"PLEASE, PLEASE THINK OF DENNIS."

OUT all NIGHT

IN THE MORNING I WAS NOT FEELING CALM ABOUT DENNIS THE BABY AND THE SPRAWLED LADY SAYING,"OW. OH. MY HEAD. MY HEAD." I ASKED HER COULD SHE DO ME A FAVOR OF EXPLAINING TO MY MOM WHERE I WAS ALL NIGHT. SHE SAID,"CIGS. CIGS. MY CIGS." AND I GOT THEM FOR HER AND THEN SHE SAID NO. SHE WOULDN'T.

WAIT! WAIT! DON'T GO YET. WHAT'S YOUR NAME?

FREDDIE.

UH, FREDDIE?

YEAH?

THINK YOU COULD MAKE COFFEE?

WAH WA

SO WALKING HOME I WAS VERY NERVOUS ABOUT MOM. I WAS PRACTICING MY WORDS TO HER. I WAS THINKING OF HER SCREAMING AT ME, THE WAY SHE LEANS AT ME SHOUTING LOUD. I DRIVE HER CRAZY. I DRIVE HER OUT OF HER HEAD. OBVIOUSLY I AM TRYING TO KILL HER. WHY? WHY DO I DO THIS TO HER?

MY SISTER MAYBONNE SAYS
WHY DO YOU PROVOKE HER?
WHEN MOM SCREAMS AT ME
SHE ALSO SCREAMS AT MY SIS-
TERS. ONCE SHE GETS MAD SHE
CAN'T STOP THE SCREAMING.
THERE IS A MOVIE CALLED "THE
SCREAMING SKULL" AND THERE
ARE SO MANY REASONS FOR
A SKULL TO SCREAM.

LADY, LADY,
PLEASE
STOP IT.

FREDDEEE
YOU KILLED MEEEE
BURNED MEEEE

FEELI
VEL

PLEASE GO
AWAY. PLEASE
PLEASE.

AND WHEN I OPEN THE BACK
DOOR MY HEART IS CHOKING
ME AND SHE IS IN THE KITCHEN
DRINKING COFFEE AND LOOKING
BORED. "YOU'RE UP EARLY" IS
HER ONLY COMMENT. SHE IS
YAWNING AND TURNING NEWS-
PAPER PAGES. "GO GET ME MY
CIGARETTES. END TABLE. FRONT
ROOM." AND THAT WAS ALL.
THAT WAS ALL SHE SAID.

WHAT?
WHAT ARE YOU
LOOKING AT
ME FOR?

MOVE IT!

BLUBBO'S BLAM

AND SO I TRIED IGNORING THE SCREAMING SKULL AND CONCENTRATING ON THE GOOD THINGS IN LIFE. LIKE EOGYRINUS THE ANCIENT LONELY AMPHIBIAN.

MOST OF HIS FRIENDS WENT TERRESTRIAL AND NEVER LOOKED BACK. I THOUGHT OF BLUBBO. HOW HE NEVER GOT A VISITOR. HOW HE BLEW HIS DAD'S HEAD OFF WITH A SHOTGUN. I ASKED HIM WHY HE DID IT.

HIS VIOLENT ACTION WASN'T PLANNED. HIS DAD HAD THEM LINED UP AND HE TOLD THEM WHAT HE WAS GOING TO DO AND HE HAD A PISTOL AND A SHOTGUN AND HE WAS VERY DRUNK AND HE SAT IN A CHAIR SCREAMING AT THEM UNTIL HE PASSED OUT AND BLUBBO GOT THE SHOTGUN AND BLAM.

MOM WAS CALLING FOR HELP. WHEN THE COPS CAME SHE TOLD THEM SHE DIDN'T KNOW WHAT GOT INTO ME.

NO ONE WOULD STAND UP FOR BLUBBO. HIS MOM WAS VERY MAD. SHE TOLD THE COPS BLUBBO KNEW HIS DAD WOULDN'T SHOOT THEM. HIS DAD DID IT ALL THE TIME, LINED THEM UP LIKE THAT AND POINTED GUNS AT THEM. JUST BLOWING OFF STEAM. HE WASN'T SERIOUS. IT HAPPENED ALL THE TIME.

DIDN'T NOBODY BELIEVE YOU, BLUBBO? DIDN'T NO ONE UNDERSTAND?

WHAT WAS THERE TO UNDERSTAND?

EOGYRINUS

PSSST! YOUNG MAN! YOU MUST STOP READING ALOUD OR I WILL REQUIRE YOU TO LEAVE THE LIBRARY

TAP TAP

DREAMY

NOW I LAY ME DOWN TO— "QUIET!" SHOUTED MOM. IT WAS THE NIGHT BEFORE SCHOOL STARTED. I HAD BEEN PRAYING TOO MUCH. THE SKULL HEADS.

AND SO I SLEPT AND DREAMED A DREAM.

AND IN MY DREAM THERE WAS A CREATURE. NOT TOO FRIENDLY, NOT TOO MEAN. HE CLOSED MY EYES AND OPENED THEM.

"GET UP, GET UP," MY SISTER SAID. A NEW DAY, ANOTHER CHANCE. THE WORLD LOOKED DIFFERENT BUT HER FACE WAS BACK.

MR FILE

THIS YEAR I'M IN ROOM NINE. MR. FILE. DREADED. FAMOUS. NO ONE WISHES FOR HIM BUT 30 DESKS ARE IN HIS CLASS AND I AM IN SEAT 14.

SURPRISE ME, PEOPLE.

GET IT RIGHT THE FIRST TIME.

SEATING CHART

THE FIRST DAY OF SCHOOL IS A MOST HOPEFUL DAY. NO ONE HAS BLACK MARKS AGAINST THEM AND THE PEOPLE HAVEN'T BEEN SORTED INTO PILES OF POPULARITY YET.

PSST. HEY.

KNOW WHAT SEAT YOU'RE IN?

THE FAG SEAT.

14 IS WHERE THE FAG SITS.

40

MR. FILE HAS A MENTHOL NOSE INHALER TUBE THAT HE CONSTANTLY PUTS IN HIS NOSTRILS. THE SMELL IS SO STRONG. THE FUMES ARE QUITE OBVIOUS FROM SEAT 14.

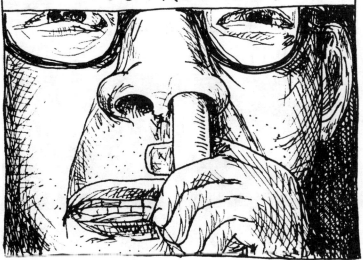

I THROW UP SO EASY. NERVOUSNESS AND CERTAIN SMELLS. ON THE FIRST DAY OF SCHOOL NATURALLY I WAS NERVOUS. MY HOPEFULNESS ENDED AT 9:17.

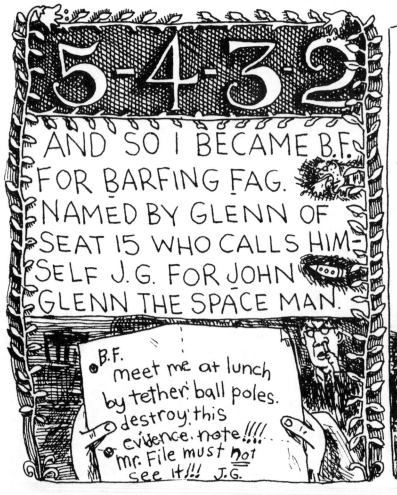

5·4·3·2

AND SO I BECAME B.F. FOR BARFING FAG. NAMED BY GLENN OF SEAT 15 WHO CALLS HIM SELF J.G. FOR JOHN GLENN THE SPACE MAN.

B.F.
meet me at lunch by tether ball poles. destroy this evidence. note!!!!.. mr. File must not see it!!! J.G.

HE SAYS WE COULD BE PARTNERS IN A CERTAIN KIND OF GAME WHERE I WANT TO DESTROY THE PLANET WITH A FLOOD OF KILLER FAG BARF AND HE MUST SAVE THE WORLD FROM ME. I THOUGHT IT SOUNDED FUN.

GLENN IS AN INTER-
ESTING SORT OF
PERSON. HE IS CON-
VINCED OF CERTAIN
THINGS. HE SAYS PLU-
TO IS CLOSER THAN
VENUS BUT NO ONE
WILL ADMIT IT.

HE SAYS HE IS 37 BUT
SMALL FOR HIS AGE
WHICH IS WHY HE IS
IDEAL FOR BEING AN
ASTRONAUT. THE FBI
GAVE HIM HIS UNDER-
COVER IDENTITY OF
4TH GRADER BUT SOON
THE WORLD WOULD
KNOW. "SOON", HE SAID.

BUDDY

THERE ARE CERTAIN PEOPLE WHO ONCE YOU BECOME FRIENDS WITH THEM THEY WILL TRY TO RULE YOUR LIFE. GLENN THE SPACE MAN IS ONE.

NO. YOU'RE GOING THIS WAY.

I DIDN'T MIND IT REALLY. HE INVITED ME OVER. I MET HIS MOM WHO MAINLY SITS IN THEIR CAR READING THRILLER BOOKS. THE ONE SHE WAS READING WAS CALLED "AX IN THE FOREHEAD."

SHE SEEMED LIKE A NICE LADY. GLENN SAID SHE STAYS IN THE CAR BECAUSE OF FBI ORDERS AND NOTHING IN HIS HOUSE IS WHAT IT SEEMS TO BE.

SHHH... THAT GIRL THERE? SUPPOSED TO BE MY SISTER?

MECHANICAL.

THE MOST INNOCENT-LOOKING THINGS CAN BLOW YOUR FACE OFF IF YOU TOUCH THEM THE WRONG WAY. SPIES ARE EVERYWHERE. "BE COOL. BE COOL," SAID GLENN THE SPACE-MAN. "WE ARE BEING WATCHED."

BUG OFF GLENN!

SEE?

MR. SPACEMAN

FATHERS ARE A MYSTERY. THEY HAVE DIFFERENT METHODS. SOME CAN TURN INVISIBLE. MR. FILE SAID WRITE AN ESSAY ABOUT YOUR FATHER.

HE SAID EVERYTHING YOU NEED TO KNOW ABOUT SOMEONE IS IN THE DESCRIPTION OF THEIR FATHER. HE TOLD US THIS AFTER IT WAS TOO LATE. AFTER WE HAD ALREADY PASSED OUR PAPERS FORWARD.

RED DEVIL BRAND

FIRE BALLS

My Dad invents fantastic candy that the people love.

GLENN THE SPACE MAN GOT VERY UPSET AND FORGOT TO RAISE HIS HAND BEFORE HE SPOKE. "MR. FILE," HE SAID, "I NEED MY STORY BACK." THE WORLD STOOD STILL.

MR. FILE! ITS A MATTER OF NATIONAL SECURITY!

SERIOUSLY.

MR. FILE LOOKED UNTIL HE FOUND ESSAY #15. "SEE HERE, CLASS," HE SAID. "I WILL SHOW YOU WHAT I MEAN." STORIES OF A FATHER ARE VERY PERSONAL. MR. FILE CLEARED HIS THROAT AND BEGAN TO READ.

MY DAD INVENTS FANTAS--

WAIT...

WHAT THE..?

GOOD LORD!

THIS IS INSANE!

OVERHEARD

WHAT DID GLENN WRITE IN HIS PAPER THAT MADE MR. FILE GET SO UPSET?

LIES!!! LIES!!!

OUTRAGEOUS CLAIMS!

R-R-R-I-N-G!!!

THE BELL RANG FOR RECESS BUT GLENN THE SPACEMAN HAD TO STAY. PEOPLE MADE A CIRCLE AROUND ME ON THE PLAYFIELD. "HE'S YOUR FRIEND," THEY SAID, "TELL US."

"I'M NOT HIS FRIEND," I SAID, "I JUST KNOW HIM." IT WAS TRUE.

BUT IF I HAD KNOWN HE WAS STANDING RIGHT THERE, I NEVER WOULD HAVE SAID IT.

FOURTH COUSIN

SOME PEOPLE GET SAD WHEN YOU HURT THEIR FEELINGS. SOME GET VERY MAD. GLENN THE SPACEMAN ISSUES DEATH WARRANTS.

HEY.

I'VE INFORMED MY PEOPLE, FAG-O.

WHAP!

"WHAT ABOUT YOUR DAD?" HE WHISPERED. "HE AS BIG A FAG AS YOU?" GLENN'S DAD INVENTED CERTAIN CANDIES. VERY FAMOUS ONES LIKE MILK JAWS.

THEY WANT TO KNOW WHO YOU ARE WORKING FOR.

HEY.

TAKE ME TO YOUR LEADER.

LIKE JOLLY JIM'S P-NUT WADS. LIKE BING-BONG ROLLS AND KANSAS RED SCREAMIES. "WHAT ABOUT YOUR DAD?" SAID GLENN. "THINK HE'S COMING TO YOUR FUNERAL? THINK HE'LL SHOW UP?"

YOU'RE FREAKING, AREN'T YOU?

I GOT YOU FREAKED NOW.

GLENN, I--

TOO LATE, FAG.

MILK

MR. FILE DISPUTED THE CLAIMS MADE IN GLENN'S PAPER. HE KNEW THE INVENTOR OF THOSE CANDIES. HIS 3RD COUSIN TWICE REMOVED NAMED LEON FABULOSO. "YEAH," SAID GLENN THE SPACEMAN, "MY DAD."

THIS CANNOT BE!!

EXCEPT IT IS, MR. FILE.

MY VISITOR

I NEED TO TELL YOU ABOUT A CERTAIN KIND OF MONSTER, THE NIGHT MONSTER. OBVIOUSLY MY IMAGINATION. OBVIOUSLY. OBVIOUSLY.

THAT DUDE THAT'S BUGGING YOU? THAT GLENN DUDE? I'LL KICK HIS BUTT OFF IF YOU SAY FOR ME TO. THAT DUDE IS A CHUMP!

SOMETIMES HE IS ON THE OTHER SIDE OF THE WORLD CATCHING CHILDREN UP IN DIRTY SACKS AND RUNNING THROUGH THE THORN BUSHES, RUNNING THROUGH THE GOAT YARDS AND DOWN DRY ROADS THROUGH THE VILLAGE.

YOU DON'T GOT TO FEEL WEIRD FOR A GIRL STICKING UP FOR YOU, FREDDIE. I'M JUST NATURALLY MORE VIOLENT.

THE WORLD SPINS BUT HE STAYS IN ONE PLACE GALLOPING. IMAGINATION. OBVIOUSLY. OBVIOUSLY. HE HAS CAUGHT ME UP IN HIS DIRTY SACK AND I HAVE VISITED WITH CHILDREN OF MANY NATIONS. THERE ARE BETTER PLACES TO MEET PEOPLE. I HAVE SMELLED BETTER SMELLS.

FREDDIE. YOU OK?

YOU DREAM HIM AGAIN? HE CATCH YOU LAST NIGHT?

BECAUSE THE NIGHT MONSTER IS ROTTING. HE IS ROTTING, ROTTING, BUT HE WILL NOT ROT AWAY. MAYBE YOU HAVE SEEN HIM IN YOUR BEDROOM. HE IS IMAGINATION, OBVIOUSLY, OBVIOUSLY. BUT MAYBE YOU HAVE SEEN HIM WHEN ALL THE SUN IS GONE.

FREDDIE! FREDDIE! YOU OK?

CITY OF GOLD

MR. FILE IS DEEPLY DISTURBED BY THE INFORMATION OF GLENN BEING HIS DISTANT RELATION. HE SAYS THERE MUST BE SOME MISTAKE BUT GLENN BROUGHT IN BOXES OF HIS DAD'S FAMOUS CANDIES FOR PROOF.

ORIGINAL FLAVOR!!

GOOD GRAVY! IT'S AUTOGRAPHED!!

TOLD MY DAD ABOUT YOU, MR FILE. HE SAID BRING YOU THESE.

MILK JAWS

AND AS A SPECIAL DELIGHT HE BROUGHT IN A NEW CANDY THE WORLD HAS NEVER SEEN, JUST INVENTED BY HIS FATHER, CALLED LEMON SPASMS OR CITRUS TWITCHERS, HE HADN'T DECIDED YET.

HE SAID WOULD YOU HONOR HIM WITH YOUR OPINION OF THEM.

INDEED!! OH!! OH!! INDEED!! INDEED!!

GLENN'S FATHER SAID HE WOULD LEAVE IT UP TO MR. FILE. LEMON SPASMS, CITRUS TWITCHERS OR ANYTHING ELSE MR. FILE MIGHT COME UP WITH. MR. FILE WAS SO OBVIOUSLY HONORED.

PLEASE TELL YOUR FATHER I SHALL NOT DISAPPOINT HIM!

THIS CALLS FOR A NEW NOSE TUBE!

SNIFFY SNIFF SNIFF!

AHHH!

"TEACHER'S PET" ISN'T WORDS ENOUGH TO EXPLAIN GLENN'S NEW SITUATION. MR. FILE SAW A FUTURE. HE SAID CANDY WAS IN HIS BLOOD. HE SAID TURN TO P. 63 AND READ TO OURSELVES ABOUT THE SPANIARDS. PONCE DE LEON, CORONADO, DE SOTO, CORTEZ. HE SAID READ THE WHOLE CHAPTER. HE NEEDED TIME TO CONCENTRATE.

SKURVY-TURVYS...

THAT'S IT. PURE GENIUS!

55

CLOUD SHADOW

YOU CAN BUY A LOT WITH THE RIGHT CANDY. A LOT OF DREAMS. A LOT OF NIGHTMARES. "IT'S WAR," SAID GLENN THE SPACEMAN. "MY PEOPLE VS. YOUR PEOPLE. ASTRONAUTS VS. FAGS."

"I SURRENDER," WAS MY RESPONSE. "THEN YOU ARE MY PRISONER." SAID GLENN. "AFTER SCHOOL. WAIT FOR ME BY THE MONKEY BARS." MR. FILE SAID, "PAGE 171 IN YOUR SCIENCE BOOK." THE STORY OF CLOUDS. MY BOOK SMELLS LIKE PERFUME. SOMEONE DREW A BIRD POOPING ON THE CUMULUS CLOUD.

WHAT DID YOUR FATHER THINK OF MY SUGGESTION?

SUGGESTION?

SKURVY-TURVYS.

OH. YEAH. UM... GENIUS. YOU ARE ONE.

SUDDENLY INSPIRATION IS EVERY WHERE!

CLASS? WOULD YOU ENJOY A CANDY CALLED "CREAMY-CRISP CUMULUS CRAWLIES"?

OR WHAT ABOUT "NIMBUS NUT-KNOCKERS"?

THE MOISTURE OF THE AIR CONDENSES AND FORMS CLOUDS. MANY KINDS SO VISIBLE DURING THE DAY. NIMBUS, CUMULONIMBUS, CIRRUS AND STRATUS. "YOU ARE MY PRISONER OF WAR," SAID GLENN. "CERTAIN THINGS WILL HAPPEN TO YOU." WE WERE IN HIS BASEMENT. CERTAIN THINGS DID.
OK.
YOU'RE A GIRL. PRETEND YOU ARE A GIRL AND A SPY AND YOU HAVE BETRAYED ME. PUT YOUR HANDS BEHIND YOUR BACK.

"IF YOU TELL," SAID GLENN. "IF YOU EVEN SAY A WORD." MOISTURE RISES FROM THE OCEAN AND THE RIVERS. IT RISES FROM WADING POOLS AND THE DEAD SEA, ESPECIALLY THE DEAD SEA. TO FLOAT AWAY, TO BREAK APART AND FLOAT AWAY. YES. YES. CIRRUS IS MY PICK. A MILE HIGH ABOVE THE EARTH AND NEVER COMING BACK HERE.
DO YOU KNOW WHAT TIME IT IS? YOU MIND TELLING ME WHERE THE HELL YOU'VE BEEN?

THE END OF

MY SISTER MARLYS CAN FIGHT BACK. IF SHE GOT TAKEN PRISONER SHE WOULD KILL THE COMMANDER AND RULE THE PLATOON. THE MOVIE WOULD BE ABOUT HER. I'D BE THE ONE WHO GETS BLOWN UP BY A LAND MINE BEFORE THE FIRST COMMERCIAL.

GLENN THE EVIL MAN FROM SPACE WOULD STAY ALIVE UNTIL THE LAST FIVE MINUTES. THERE WOULD BE A SHOWDOWN. EVIL VS. GOOD IN A FIGHT TO THE FINISH. GLENN WOULD LOSE. HE WOULD DIE. I IMAGINED ALL OF THIS DURING MY TIME OF BEING PRISONER IN HIS BASEMENT. YOU EVER KNOW A KID THAT DIED?

IT WAS YOUR IDEA. I HATE WHAT YOU MAKE ME DO TO YOU.

GET AWAY FROM ME.

WHAT'S WRONG WITH YOU? I SAID LEAVE. GO HOME.

HE'S HERE.

HIS SEAT WAS EMPTY AND I WAS GLAD. I WAS SO SICK OF "BASEMENT PRISONER." AFTER LUNCH CAME MR. FILE SNORKING AND BAWLING WITH AN ANNOUNCEMENT. A DEAR BOY. A DEAR, DEAR, DEAR CLASSMATE. OUR OWN DEAR GLENN PASSED AWAY LAST NIGHT. MR. FILE'S CANDY-COLORED FUTURE CRUMBLED.

"I'M DREAMING THIS I'M DREAMING THIS," I WHISPERED AND SOME PEOPLE LOOKED MY WAY. CAUSE OF DEATH AT THIS TIME UNKNOWN. CAUSE OF DEATH NOT KNOWN UNTIL THAT NIGHT WHEN THE AUTOPSY MAN FOUND IT. IN THE THROAT OF GLENN A CHOKER OBJECT. A PEANUT. FOUND A PEANUT. FOUND A PEANUT.

WHAT I KNOW

THEY SENT ME TO THE OFFICE BECAUSE I COULD NOT STOP SINGING IT: "FOUND A PEANUT, FOUND A PEANUT, FOUND A PEANUT JUST NOW." MR. FILE WAS ESPECIALLY HARSH ON ME.

OUT! OUT! OUT OF MY CLASSROOM, YOU SICK BEING!

GLENN'S DEATH BY PEANUT. BY PEANUT. FOUND A PEANUT. THE NIGHT THEY FOUND GLENN, THE NIGHT MONSTER FOUND ME. HE HAD GLENN IN HIS SACK. "YOU OR HIM? YOU OR HIM?" SAID THE NIGHT MONSTER'S HORROR HOLE. "HIM," I SAID. "HIM, HIM FOR SURE."

FREDERICK, PRINCIPAL COFFRAY WILL SEE YOU NOW.

GLENN'S FATHER WAS NOT AT THE FUNERAL AND HE WAS NOT LEON FABULOSO AND HE NEVER INVENTED CANDY. HE WAS A DENTIST WITH VERY HAIRY HANDS. HE SAID HE NEEDED TO STAY AT WORK, HIS PATIENT LOAD WAS INSANE, WHILE GLENN WAS BURIED HIS FATHER CLEANED A FAT MAN'S TEETH.

NOW, I AM SURE IT'S BEEN HARD ON YOU, FREDERICK, LOSING SUCH A CLOSE FRIEND, BUT---

THE MOTHER OF GLENN LEANED HEAVILY ON MR. FILE AND THEY HAD THE TENDER EXCHANGE. SOME SEEDS WERE DROPPED IN THE POTTING MIX. I WAS THERE. THEY THOUGHT I WAS HIS BEST FRIEND. "HIM OR YOU?" SAID THE ROTTING NIGHT SHADOW-CREATURE. "HIM, HIM. HIM FOR ABSOLUTE SURE."

WHAT'S THIS MEAN, YOU NEED TIME FOR EMOTIONAL RECOVERY? STAY AT HOME?!? LIKE HELL!

OLD BUDDY

THIS CREATURE, THIS FEL-LOW (HE WANTS TO BE CALLED FELLOW, BUDDY, PAL), HE HAS ALWAYS BEEN SHOWING UP IN MY LIFE AND I HAVE ALWAYS BEEN AFRAID, FOR HE HAS POWERS MIGHTY.

GRIMLY TRUE!

IMAGINATION, IMAGINATION, YES, I KNOW, BUT THINGS CAN HAPPEN. A PEANUT. A FIRE. I DO NOT CONTROL HIM, THIS FELLOW, THIS BUDDY, THIS PAL. NOT AN IMAGINARY FRIEND. THE VERY OPPOSITE OF AN IMAGINARY FRIEND. WE WERE BORN TOGETHER.

MARLYS BELIEVES ME, BUT MY MOM, NO. SISSY, I'M JUST BEING A SISSY, I'M MORE OF A GIRL THAN MARLYS IS." THIS HAS GOT TO STOP. THAT BOY, THAT GLENN HAS BEEN DEAD TWO MONTHS NOW. THIS HAS GOT TO END!" THAT IS WHAT SHE YELLS.

NOW. <u>GO</u>. TO. <u>SLEEP</u>.

THE FELLOW KNOWS, THE FELLOW SAW, AND THEN HE KILLED GLENN WITH A PEANUT. HE KEEPS GLENN IN HIS SACK AND GLENN IS ROTTING WITH A SMILE ON HIS FACE. EVERY NIGHT I SCREAM. I AM STILL HIS PRISONER.

HERE COMES THE ☀ SUN

HERE COMES THE SUN, I AM SINGING IT OVER AND OVER IN MY BED IN THE DARKNESS BUT I CAN STILL SMELL HIM, I CAN STILL SEE HIM. HERE COMES THE SUN. HERE COMES THE SUN.

MOM SAYS I'M DREAMING IT BUT MY EYES ARE OPEN. HE IS WALKING BACK AND FORTH, HE IS LOOKING AT ME AND SHAKING HIS HEAD. PLEASE DON'T LET HIM OPEN HIS MOUTH. I DON'T WANT TO SEE HIS MOUTH. HERE COMES THE SUN. HERE COMES THE SUN.

IT'S NOT WORKING, FLOWERS, BEAUTIFUL FLOWERS AND BLUE SKY AND JESUS AND BEAUTIFUL GOD SHINE SUN AND IT'S NOT WORKING! NO-THING I AM THINKING IS WORKING! IF HE OPENS HIS MOUTH I WILL HAVE TO GO IN AGAIN AND CLEAN HIS GUTS MOM MOM I AM SCREAMING MOM MOM MOM 2+2+2+2+

SHE SAID SHE HEARD ME. SHE TOLD ME YES, SHE HEARD ME, BUT IF SHE CAME EVERY TIME I CALLED, WOULD I EVER GROW UP TO BE A MAN? SHE WAS EATING DINNER. "YOU WANT TO BE A MAN, DON'T YOU?" SHE LOOKED AT ME. "SO. NO MORE OF THIS." SHE BIT ON HER MEAT. "NO MORE OF THIS NONSENSE."

EAT.

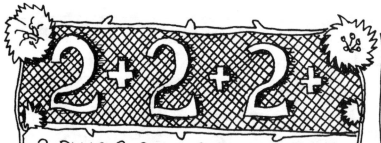

2+2+2+

2 PLUS 2 PLUS 2 PLUS 2 "FOR THE LOVE OF <u>GOD</u>!" SCREAMS MOM. MY 2 PLUS 2 PLUS 2 IS DRIVING HER NUTS, SHE WANTS ME TO STOP IT, MR. FILE WANTS ME PUT IN SPECIAL ED. IT'S WINTER.

IT'S WINTER AND GLENN'S HEAD HAS ROTTED DOWN TO HIS SKULL. SKULLS A-GAIN. OLD BUDDY BRINGS THEM IN AT NIGHT, IN HIS SACK THEY CRACK TOGETHER. 2+2+2+2. IT KEEPS OLD BUDDY FROZEN. 2+2+2+2. I HAVE TO KEEP SAYING IT. I WHISPER IT. I WHISPER IT.

2 + 2 + 2 + 2 ONWARD TO IN-FINITY. I HAVE BEEN GET-TING SINISTER HEADACHES AND IF YOU HAVE EVER HEARD A DOG WHISTLE IT HAS A SOUND THAT IS IN MY BRAINS AND WANTS TO BREAK MY GLASSES. MARLYS IS NOW BEGGING ME. STOP, FREDDIE. NO MORE MATH, FREDDIE, STOP.

SHE IS VERY WORRIED. IT IS WINTER AND COMING ON CHRISTMAS VACATION AND I AM FLUNKING EVERY-THING AND AT SCHOOL THEY ARE REVIEWING, THEY ARE DECIDING: SHOULD I BE AL-LOWED TO COME BACK AT ALL? 2+2+2+2. AT ALL.

in the dead of Morning

FIRST I AM JUST LYING UNDER
THE COVERS. MY NEW BEDROOM
IS IN THE BASEMENT. NO WIN-
DOWS. AND I ALWAYS WONDER:
WHAT TIME IS IT? IS IT STILL
NIGHT? IS IT MORNING? I
HAVE READ ABOUT ANTARCTICA.
4 MONTHS WITH NO SUN. I
JUST HEARD MOM'S FEET WALK
ACROSS THE KITCHEN.

THAT MEANS 2 HOURS BEFORE
SCHOOL. IN ANTARCTICA, I
HAVE READ THAT SOMETIMES
THE SKY IS GREEN LIKE NEW
LEAVES. MY MOM HAS HER
RADIO ON. THE SOUNDS OF BEAU-
TIFUL MUSIC IS HER RADIO STA-
TION. THE RADIO MAN SAYS, "RE-
LAX. YOU ARE LISTENING TO
THE SOUNDS OF BEAUTIFUL MU-
SIC". OF ANIMALS IN ANTARCTICA
THERE ARE PENGUINS, SEALS,
WHALES AND BIRDS.

IN THE EGG THE PENGUIN CHICK MAKES SOUNDS BEFORE IT HATCHES. THE FATHER KEEPS HIS BODY ON THE EGG AND THEN THE MOTHER DOES. IF THEY MOVE AWAY EVEN ONE INCH THE EGG WILL FREEZE. I SMELL MOM'S COFFEE. I WOULD LIKE TO GO UP AND SIT WITH HER. I WOULD LIKE TO TELL HER SHE LOOKS PRETTY BUT IN THE MORNING SHE LIKES BEING ALONE. PENGUINS TRAVEL ON BROKEN ICE.

THEY RIDE IT LIKE A BOAT ACROSS THE FREEZING WATER. IN MY COVERS I CAN DO THAT. FLOAT ON THE PITCH-BLACK DARK. I RIDE ON THE SEAS OF ANT-ARCTICA. THE ROSS SEA. THE WEDDELL SEA. I RELAX TO THE SOUNDS OF BEAUTIFUL MUSIC AND HER FEET WALK BACK AND FORTH ABOVE ME UNTIL THE FRONT DOOR OPENS AND SHUTS. AND THEN HER CAR STARTS. AND THEN IT IS TIME TO SWIM BACK TO LAND.

69

SICK LEAVE

THE BASEMENT IS BAD FOR CERTAIN LUNGS. THERE ARE SPORE CREATURES GROWING. IT IS COLD. IT IS WET. SHE PUT ME THERE SO EVERYONE ELSE COULD SLEEP BECAUSE MY COUNTING AND YELLING AGAINST OLD BUDDY WAS DISRUPTIVE.

SEE?

FEVER.

DAMN IT, 102°.

HELL.

AND NOW WITH ONLY 3 DAYS LEFT BEFORE WINTER VACATION I AM VERY SICK. MOM IS SMOKING AND SAYING SHE CAN'T MISS WORK. I LOOK AT HER CIGARETTE AND SEE A TINY BURNING FACE MOVING LIPS AT ME. MOM CAN'T MISS WORK. MY SISTER MAYBONNE WILL HAVE TO STAY HOME WITH ME.

"WE HAVE TO EAT," SAYS MOM. MAYBONNE SAYS, "JUST GO. IT'S OK." BANG GOES THE FRONT DOOR. MOM'S CAR DRIVES AWAY. I'M ON THE COUCH. MY SISTER MAYBONNE IS ON THE PHONE CALLING HER FRIEND BRENDA.

HI. BRENDA THERE?

HEY. IT'S ME.

GOTTA STAY HOME AND WATCH FREDDIE.

YEAH.

SKIP WITH ME.

C'MON. PLEASE?

PLEASE? JUST COME OVER, 'K?

'K? BREN-DA... C'MON.

MARLYS MAKES HER LUNCH, THEN PUTS HER COAT ON AND HER MITTENS. SHE SAYS, "YOU FAKING, FREDDIE? SOMETIMES I FAKE." I SHAKE MY HEAD NO, NO, NO, AND THEN VERY QUICKLY I AM ASLEEP. IN A LIGHT ROOM WITH WINDOWS IT IS SO, SO EASY TO SLEEP.

FORBIDS

BRENDA AND MY SISTER, THEY TOOK SOME PILL. A PILL THEY SPLIT AND ARGUED OVER, TRYING TO GET THE HALVES EXACT, IT WAS SO IMPORTANT THAT THEY WERE EXACT. THEY THOUGHT I WAS ASLEEP.

AND SOMETIMES I WAS. THEY CALL IT DRIFTING, PARTLY FLOATING INTO NOTHING. I HEARD THEM SPEAKING. "FEEL IT? DO YOU? DO YOU?" THEY WERE SMOKING AND THE BLUE EXHALES HUNG AND TWISTED WITH THE DUST IN THE SLANTING LIGHT.

"NOW?" SAID BRENDA. "NO," SAID MAYBONNE. SHE WAS COMPLAINING ABOUT MOM, HOW MOM SAID, "FORBID." MOM SAID, "I <u>FORBID</u> YOU TO SHAVE YOUR LEGS," AND THEN BRENDA SAID, "<u>NOW</u> DO YOU?" MY SISTER SAID, "IT'S A BURN. IT'S BOGUS." AND I DRIFTED.

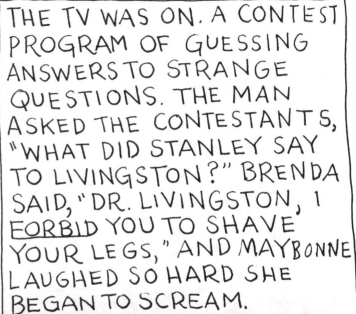

THE TV WAS ON. A CONTEST PROGRAM OF GUESSING ANSWERS TO STRANGE QUESTIONS. THE MAN ASKED THE CONTESTANTS, "WHAT DID STANLEY SAY TO LIVINGSTON?" BRENDA SAID, "DR. LIVINGSTON, I <u>FORBID</u> YOU TO SHAVE YOUR LEGS," AND MAYBONNE LAUGHED SO HARD SHE BEGAN TO SCREAM.

HIGH

HIGH. HIGH. HIGH FEVER AND THEN HIGHER. MY SISTER AND BRENDA IN THE HALL TALKING ALL ABOUT HALLS. WHAT THEY MEAN. TALKING SO FAST.

THE AIR WAS NOT SO EASY TO BREATHE AND I FELT SO DIZZY WITH EYELIDS HOT. MY BONES RUBBER HOT. THE CEILING MOVED LIKE A STOMACH. HIGH. VERY HIGH. 106°, 107.°

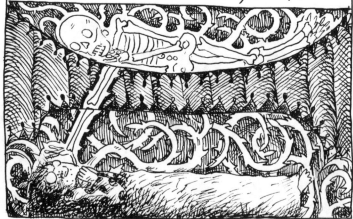

AFTER HALLS BRENDA MENTIONED WALLS AND MY SISTER TOUCHED THE WALLS, AND I WATCH, I AM WATCHING HER AND SHE SHRINKS, SHE BECOMES TEENY-TINY MINISCULE AND A CIRCLE OF BLACKNESS BEGAN TO SWALLOW HER.

AND THAT IS ALL. I COULD HEAR HER BUT HIS MOUTH, OLD BUDDY'S MOUTH CLOSED AROUND ME AND I LOST MY VIEW. HOW HOT. HOW HIGH THE TEMPERATURE AND HOW LITTLE AIR WAS INSIDE OF OLD BUDDY. I JUST COULD NOT BREATHE.

TINY WORLD

IN THE CHIP OF PILL MY
SISTER SWALLOWED,
THERE WAS A LITTLE
WORLD, AND IN THIS
WORLD I WAS BURNING.

AND BECAUSE OF
THIS SHE WAS
FREAKING AND SHE
WAS PEAKING AND
HER WORLD COLLI-
DED WITH BRENDA'S
WORLD, WHERE I WAS
DROWNING.

AND MY WORLD WIGGLED ITS FINGERS AT THEM AND WOBBLED THE AIR LIKE SHIMMERING HEAT ABOVE A BLACK TAR ROAD AND MY SISTER BEGAN TO PRAY.

"JESUS, JESUS, PLEASE HELP ME COME DOWN, OH GOD, PLEASE HELP, I NEED TO COME DOWN." BRENDA WAS SHRIEKING, "HE'S DYING! HE'S SINKING! HE DOESN'T HAVE AIR!" FROM INSIDE OLD BUDDY I HEARD IT ALL.

FREDDIE?

What happened next I cannot know because I died, I was so dead, there was no hope for me.

Marlys says that when she came home she saw May-Bonne and Brenda running figure eights in the freezing front yard. They weren't wearing coats and their skin looked yellow.

IT WAS FOR THEM THAT MARLYS DIALED ZERO, HELLO OPERATOR, THIS IS AN EMERGENCY. I CAN'T SAY WHAT MARLYS SAW WHEN SHE LOOKED AT ME. SHE WILL NOT TELL ME BUT THERE WAS OLD BLOOD INTERNAL.

AND IN THE HOSPITAL THE DOCTORS BROUGHT A PERSON BACK ALIVE WHO WAS NOT ME. AND THEY CALLED HIM BY MY NAME AND HE AN-SWERED THEM. AND I WATCHED. AND HE DID NOT KNOW I EXISTED.

WATCH ME

AND WHEN THE NEW YEAR CAME, AND THEN SOME WEEKS PASSED, THE NEW BOY WALKED TO MY SCHOOL AND TOOK MY SEAT. PEOPLE STARED AT HIM.

HEY! HEY!

MY CHAIR! GET OFF!!

MR. FILE SAID, "A-HEM, A-HEM." HE SAID, "FREDDIE," AND FREDDIE, THE NEW, STRANGE FREDDIE, THE ME THAT WAS NOT ME, SAID, "YES, SIR?" AND PEOPLE STARED AT HIM HARDER.

"FREDDIE," SAID MR. FILE, YOU ARE IN THE WRONG ROOM. DIDN'T ANYONE TELL YOU?" AND SPAZVILLE WAS THE RIGHT ROOM. RETARDATION CORNERS, ROOM 12, "SPECIAL ED", IS WHAT MR. FILE SAID.

WHO ARE YOU?

IN THE HEAT OF SUCH A FEVER YOUR BRAINS BOIL OVER AND PART OF YOU STEAMS AWAY. EVAPORATES INTO THE AIR INVISIBLE. I WATCHED THIS NEW BOY GATHER HIS PENCILS AND BOOKS. I WATCHED THE PEOPLE STARING. THERE, BUT FOR THE GRACE OF GOD. THERE BUT FOR THE GRACE OF GOD.

WHO

THE GOOD, THE BAD AND THE UGLY. AND THE BEAUTIFUL. AND THE NICE AND THE WONDERFUL AND THE MEAN AND THE TERRIBLE, THEY ALL UNDERSTOOD MY PROBLEM WITH THE BOY WHO COULD NOT SEE ME.

YOU.

FREDDIE.

HEY, HEY.

FREDDIE.

THIS BOY, MY MOTHER LIKED VERY MUCH. SORT OF A GHOST OF A BOY WHO WAS VISIBLE BUT NOT THERE. THE GOOD, THE BAD AND THE UGLY. AND THE BEAUTIFUL. ALL UNDERSTOOD WHAT IT IS LIKE TO BE WHERE I WAS, WATCHING HIM.

HE DID NOT REMEMBER ME
OR OLD BUDDY OR THE
HEAD OF GLENN THE SPACE-
MAN. I DO NOT KNOW WHAT
HE REMEMBERED. BUT HE WAS
A VERY GOOD AND QUIET
BOY, AND HE WALKED TO
ROOM 12 WILLINGLY.

FRED-DIE!

YES.
YES.
HELLO.
YES.

MARLYS SAW HIM IN THE
HALL AND SAID HIS NAME
AND HE TURNED AND SAID,
"HELLO," AND THIS WORD,
THIS "HELLO," SCARED HER.
IT BOUNCED IN THE EMPTY
HALL AND LANDED NOWHERE.
MARLYS NOTICED. I COULD
SEE BY HER FACE THAT
SHE NOTICED I WAS NOT
THERE. WONDERFUL, TERRIBLE
MARLYS.

MAR
LYS.

INSIDE 12

INSIDE ROOM 12 I HEARD A TAMBOURINE AND SUCH A LOT OF NOISE. I WATCHED THE NOT-FREDDIE KNOCKING. THEY COULD NOT HEAR HIM. THEY WERE SINGING, "12 GATES TO THE CITY, BEAUTIFUL CITY."

HE KNOCKED AGAIN VERY SOFTLY. A PERSON DOES NOT BARGE IN. THREE GATES TO THE EAST. THREE GATES TO THE WEST. THE SINGING WAS LOUD BUT SOMEONE HEARD HIM. THE DOOR OPENED AND A CERTAIN KIND OF GIRL WAS STANDING THERE.

AND MRS. TEACHER DID NOT STOP THE SONG, SHE WAVED HIM INSIDE, HE FOLLOWED THE GIRL, SPAZ-EYES GIGI WAS HER NAME. THREE GATES TO THE NORTH, THREE GATES TO THE SOUTH. SHE SANG IT WITH ONE EYE ON HIM, AND THE OTHER WIBBLE-WOBBLED ALL OVER.

"12 GATES TO THE CITY, BEAUTIFUL CITY, GREAT BIG BEAUTIFUL CITY, OH MY, MY, WHAT A CITY." AND THEN THE SONG WAS OVER AND MRS. TEACHER SAID, "YOU MUST BE FREDDIE," AND GOOD FREDDIE NODDED AND LOOKED AWAY FROM WHAT HE SAW.

THE WISH WITCH

THE BAD, THE UGLY, THE DISTURBED, THE ANGRY, THE N-N-N-NERVOUS, THE FAT, THE SO-DIRTY. THE WEIRD. THE SPASTIC THEY SAID, "WELCOME, FREDDIE." AND HE LOOKED DOWN. IT WAS NOT POLITE TO PUT YOUR EYES UPON THESE THINGS,

ANYWHERE HE WANTED TO SIT, IS WHAT MRS. TEACHER SAID. IT WAS READING TIME. THE HORRIBLE CHILDREN GATHERED ROUND HER. FREDDIE STAYED BACK. A FAIRY TALE. A VERY WICKED WITCH WHO LIVED UNDER THE SEA.

A CERTAIN KIND OF GIRL CAME TO HER WITH A WISH. A BEAUTIFUL SWIMMING KIND OF GIRL, A SINGING SORT OF GIRL. THE HORRIBLE WITCH SAID YES. YES I WILL GRANT YOU YOUR WISH IF YOU WILL LET ME CUT OFF YOUR TONGUE. HOW BAD DID THIS SINGING GIRL WANT HER WISH?

MRS. TEACHER ASKED IF ANYONE COULD GUESS WHAT THE GIRL WANTED? BECAUSE THE WITCH PLANNED TO GOBBLE DOWN THE SINGING TONGUE, SHE TOLD THE GIRL THIS. AND THE GIRL SAID THAT GETTING HER WISH WOULD BE WORTH IT. WHAT WOULD THAT WISH BE? SPAZ-EYES GIGI RAISED HER HAND.

NEW BUDDY

WE DID NOT HEAR SPAZ-EYES GIGI'S ANSWER BECAUSE THE FIRE BELL RANG. I WATCHED GOOD FREDDIE WALK SINGLE FILE WITH THE OTHERS. THERE WERE TWO CREATURES BEHIND HIM. OLD BUDDY WAS ONE. BUT WHO WAS THIS OTHER?

THIS OTHER COULD SEE ME. HE LOOKED STRAIGHT AT ME. HE SAID, "HEY BABA-BUBBA!" HE SAID, "ROCKA-SAGGY-BABY-BUBBA-SHAGGY-BABA-BOO." HE POINTED AT THE GOOD FREDDIE AND SAID, "BABY-ROCKA-SAD-SHAGGY-BABA-SABA-BABA-BOO." OLD BUDDY SLINKED AWAY AND JOINED THE SHADOWS.

BABA.

SHAGGY.

BOO

88

IT BEGAN TO RAIN AND THE STARING PEOPLE SHIVERED. SO MANY EYEBALLS ON THE SPECIAL ED LINE. SOMEONE SAID TO MARLYS, "HEY, THERE'S YOUR BROTHER, FREDDIE." AND MARLYS ACTED DEAF AND MARLYS WENT BLIND TO BROTHERS. "HEE-HEE," SAID SOMEONE. "DO IT RUN IN YOUR FAMILY? DO IT?" HEE-HEE-HEE."

THREE BELLS RANG AND WE WENT INSIDE. STORY TIME WAS OVER. IT WAS TIME FOR LUNCH. SO I DID NOT KNOW WHAT WISH THE SINGING UNDERSEA GIRL MADE AFTER THE WITCH ATE HER TONGUE. BUT I WAS THINKING THAT MAYBE SHE HAD A BROTHER LIKE ME.

SABA SISTER

"YOU'RE NOT FREDDIE," SAID MARLYS TO THE BOY. SHE CREPT INTO HIS ROOM AND SAT ON HIS BED AND THEY SAT IN THE MOONLIGHT. "WHERE IS FREDDIE AT?" THE BOY SHRUGGED.

"THAT THING GOT HIM," SAID MARLYS, "THAT IMAGINARY THING GOT HIM. OLD BUDDY DID. RIGHT?" THE BOY SHRUGGED AGAIN. "I DON'T LIKE YOU," SAID MARLYS, AND SHE WENT BACK TO BED.

THE ME OF ME FOLLOWED HER. I SAID, "MARLYS, MARLYS," AND SAT CLOSE, BUT SHE COULD NOT SEE OR HEAR ME. IT WAS THE MIDDLE OF THE NIGHT AND SHE WAS THINKING. SOMETHING HAD CAUGHT ME UP AND SHE KNEW IT. JUST BECAUSE THE PROBLEM WAS IMAGINARY DID NOT MEAN IT WAS NOT REAL. SHE STARTED TO WHISPER.

BABY-BABA-ROCKA-SHAGGY-MAMA-BABA-SABA-SISTER-BROTHER-BABA-DOCTOR-SHAGGY-BACKA-BABA-BUBBA-BABY-BOO.

IS THAT IT?

THE BABA MAN, THE ROCKA-SHAGGY-BABA FELLOW CAST HIS SABA-BABA SHADOW ON THE SAGGY-BUBBA WALL. MARLYS WHISPERED OUT HIS LONG NAME AGAIN AND SUDDENLY I FELT SO SLEEPY. AND SUDDENLY I FELL ASLEEP TUMBLING.

SABU BABA

AT BREAKFAST MARLYS SAID, "EXCUSE ME, FREDDIE, BUT WHO IS BABY-BABA-ROCKA-SHAGGY-MAMA-BABA-SABA-SISTER-BROTHER-BABA-DOCTOR-SHAGGY-BACKA-BABA-BUBBA-BABY-BOO?" MOM SCREAMED, "NO! I FORBID YOU TO SAY HIS NAME IN MY HOUSE!"

THE ROOM TWIRLED A LITTLE AND THEN WENT DARK. WHEN THE LIGHT CAME BACK I WAS SEEING OUT OF FREDDIE'S EYE HOLES AT THE SITUATION. MOM WAS SLAPPING MARLYS AND I WAS ON THE FLOOR AND MAYBONNE WAS SAYING, "MARLYS, YOU ARE SO STUPID! MARLYS, YOU IDIOT!"

I WAS LAYING ON THE FLOOR AND MY BODY WAS SO VERY STRETCH-STRETCHY. MY MOUTH SAID, "MAMA-BABA!" IT SAID, "SHAGGY-BAGGY-BABA-MAMA!" MOM WHACKED MARLYS HARD AND HER LIP WAS BLEEDING. MY SISTER GOT A BLOODY LIP AND I REMEMBERED HIM.

DOLLS. NO PLAYING WITH DOLLS! FREDDIE IF I CATCH YOU ONE MORE TIME! GIVE ME THAT! DAMN YOU! GIVE IT TO ME! DAMN YOU! COME BACK HERE! FREDDIE! FREDDIE! FREDDIE! WE RAN TOGETHER INTO THE DARKNESS TO GET FREE.

STRANGE [LUCK]

CHIMNEY SWEEP. DO YOU KNOW WHAT IT MEANS? IT MEANS LUCK. SO SAID THE STRANGE LADY WHO MADE HIM FOR ME. A LADY WHO WAS RUN OUT OF TOWN.

"UGLY," IS WHAT MOM SAID. "THAT THING IS HORRIBLE!" BUT MARLYS SAID I SCREAM AND SCREAM AND SCREAM WHEN MOM TRIES TO TAKE HIM. A BLACK VELVET FACE MADE FROM SOMEONE'S OLD DRESS. "WITCH," SAID MOM ABOUT THE LADY. "RAG-PICKER."

YOU THE MENDING LADY?

MMMM.

HEAR YOU DO FINE WORK.

MMMM.

SAY YOU CAN DO INVISIBLE REWEAVING.

MMMM.

GOT THIS JACKET HERE WITH A BAD TEAR.

MMMM.

MARLYS SAID AT NIGHT I COULD NOT SLEEP WITHOUT HIM. SHE WAS HOLDING ICE AGAINST HER SWOLLEN LIP. MOM WAS GONE TO WORK. MAYBONNE SAID MARLYS JUST LIKED TO MAKE MOM MAD.

HOW MUCH YOU COST ME TO FIX THAT?

WHAT YOU WILL PAY.

YOU ASKING ME?

MM.MMM

"YOU TALKED TO HIM," SAID MARLYS. "HE TALKED BACK IN SABU-BABA. HIS LANGUAGE. YOU TAUGHT ME IT. SAGA – BACKA – SHAGGY." MY MOUTH OPENED AND HIS NAME CAME TUMBLING. MY FRIEND. MY FRIEND. MY FRIEND.

YOU MAKE THAT DOLL?

MMMM.

HOW MUCH?

HE DON'T WANT YOU. HE LOOK FOR LITTLE BOY YET.

M. ILLNESS

"WHAT'S GOING TO HAPPEN, IS--" MAYBONNE COUGHED ON HER ILLEGAL WINSTON. "YOU CAN'T EVEN SMOKE," SAID MARLYS. "WHAT'S GOING TO HAPPEN IS YOU ARE GOING TO MAKE MOM SO MAD THAT SHE WILL--" MAYBONNE COUGHED AGAIN.

BRENDA CAME UP THE BACK STEPS. "C'MON," SHE SAID. MAYBONNE GRABBED HER PURSE AND LEFT HER BOOKS ON THE TABLE. IN A MINUTE SHE WAS BLOCKS AWAY. ME AND MARLYS WERE ALONE AT THE TABLE. "YOU GOT MENTAL PROBLEMS," SHE SAID. "NO OFFENSE."

96

"I'M NOT SUPPOSED TO TELL YOU. MOM THOUGHT IT WENT AWAY." SHE DRANK SOME MILK. "PERSONALLY I ADMIRE YOUR MENTAL PROBLEMS." I SAID, "ABU-SHIB-BY-BABA." SHE SAID, "YOU'RE WELCOME."

AND IN THE ICE-COLD AIR OF THE MORNING WE WALKED TO SCHOOL. A BOY FROM HER CLASS NAMED MULLARD CAUGHT UP WITH US AND SAID, "WHO GAVE YOU THE FAT LIP, HA-HA-HA, THE FAG? THE RETARDED FAG DO IT?" MARLYS KICKED HIS LEG AND HE KNOCKED HER DOWN. A SAFETY PATROL BLEW HIS WHISTLE AND THE WORLD WENT DARK.

97

BAD CALL

"PLEASE DON'T, PLEASE." MARLYS WAS CRYING AND MAKING PRAYER HANDS TO THE PRINCIPAL WHO WAS DIALING HIS TELEPHONE. MULLARD WAS GETTING STITCHES AT THE HOSPITAL. A HUMAN BITE IS WORSE THAN A DOG BITE. WAY WORSE.

TAKE OFF YOUR COATS AND HANG THEM THERE.

DON'T CALL HER. WE'LL DO ANYTHING," SAID MARLYS. "RIGHT? RIGHT, FREDDIE?" "DIG IT," I SAID, "SIBBY-ROCKA-SHAGGY! PRINCIPAL CAN-YOU-DIG-IT-BABA! SHAGGY!" IT WAS ME WHO BIT MULLARD. IT WAS LIKE BITING SILLY PUTTY. SHAGGY! VERY-BABU-SABA! "MAY I SPEAK WITH MRS.----" MAMU-SABU WAS ON HER WAY.

"DEAD," SAID MARLYS AS WE WAITED IN THE OFFICE. "WE ARE. YOU AND ME ARE." MAMU CAME IN SHRIEKY-BABU, VERY SCREAMY-SABU, YANKED MARLYS UP SO HARD HER GLASSES FLEW ACROSS THE ROOM. PRINCIPAL DIGGY-BOO PUT HIS HANDS OUT SAYING, "NOW, NOW." BUT SHE HAD MARLYS OUT THE DOOR.

BABA MRS. SECRETARY WAS SHAGGY MOUTH OPEN WIDE. PRINCIPAL SHIGGY-DIGGY WAS SABABA. AND ME? BABA-SHIMMY-SHAGGY-BOO? I WAS GLAD I BIT HIM. REAL, REAL, GLAD, BABY-BUBBA. CAN YOU DIG IT? "CHOMP," SAID THE FAG. "CHOMP!" SAID EL FAGTASTICO.

HEE-HEE

YOU THINK THIS IS-- FUNNY?!!

EL FAGTASTICO

"I AM EL FAGTASTICO!" WAS MY BREAKFAST TABLE ANNOUNCEMENT. MY MOM SAID, "WHAT?!" I SAID, "BABA-MAMU!" SHE YELLED, "DON'T CALL ME THAT!" I SAID, "YOU'RE A LADY, AND A LADY CAN BE A LADY, AND I'M A LADY!"

WHOO-WHOO!

HEE-HEE!

SHHH!

LAA-LAA!

"WHEN COLUMBUS TOLD PEOPLE THE WORLD WAS ROUND SOME PEOPLE THOUGHT HE MEANT LIKE A PANCAKE. EL FAGTASTICO LIVES! EL FAGTASTICO, DUDE-DUDE, LADY-DUDE, LADY-LADY, DUDE-LADY, I AM ALL OF THESE THINGS!" "YOU ARE NOT!" SHOUTED MOTHER.

HOLY GOD!

UM, TRY TO MAINTAIN, FREDDIE. 'K?

"YOU ARE HURTING ME!" SCREAMS MOTHER. WHEN THE WORLD WAS BORN SO ROUND, DID IT HURT THE UNIVERSE? MOTHER LOCKS HERSELF IN THE BATHROOM. MAYBONNE IS SLIGHTLY FLYING. SHE SAYS SHE IS CRASHING AND THAT SHE GETS THE ROUNDNESS OF MY INFORMATION BUT PLEASE SHUT UP.

HOOPA HOOPA!

I'M CHI-CHI-BA-NANA, BABA!

WEE-WEE!

I DREAMED I WENT SQUARE-DANCING IN MY MAIDEN-FORM BRA.

OH FREDDIE

NO!

SSHHH!

DON'T

MARLYS SAYS SHE IS A DUDE-DUDE, LADY-DUDE, DUDE-LADY, LADY-LADY, AND I SAY, "YOU FORGOT FAG-DUDE AND FAG-LADY, SABA-SISTER!" MAYBONNE SAYS MARLYS IS THE CAUSE OF IT ALL AND I SAY, "THANK YOU, MARLYS!" THEN Shhh! Shhh! THE BATHROOM DOOR OPENS AND HERE COME THE FLAT FEET OF THE QUEEN OF SPAIN.

WHY?!!

101

STUNTMAN!

IN FEBRUARY SHE QUIT TALKING TO ME. "THE SINS OF THE FATHER," WAS THE LAST THING SHE SAID. DAD WAS A FAG. IS, WAS, I CANNOT TELL YOU. I DO NOT ACTUALLY KNOW HIM. IN THE FUTURE, FOR A JOB, I SHALL BE A STUNTMAN.

I SHALL JUMP FROM HUNDRED-FOOT TOWERS. I SHALL TANGLE WITH WILD BOARS AND MAN-EATING SHARKS. I WILL MAKE SO MANY HAIR-RAISING ESCAPES. THE WORLD WILL REMEMBER EL FAGTASTICO, THE INCREDIBLY INCREDIBLE STUNTMAN, THE FEARLESS FAG.

THE INCREDIBLY INCREDIBLE STUNTMAN! EL FAGTASTICO! — His actual life

Lookout man ITS A BomB!

and I am holding it!

Yes I know

GAngsters threw him down stairs!

you dirty rat you killed my brother

ahhhh!

He got shot off the roof By the Marshal!

this town aint bigenough for both of us.

BLAM BLAM!

←fake bullet holes

102

I WILL WRITE A BOOK ON MY LIFE. IT SHALL HAVE 779 THRILLING PAGES AND 900 ACTION DRAWINGS. SO FAR I ONLY HAVE 4 THRILLING PAGES AND 8 ACTION DRAWINGS. SHE DID NOT SPEAK TO ME IN MARCH OR APRIL. I GOT TIME.

In the lair of evil he met the killer snake!

his body was covered with killer ants! ow! ow! —ow! —ow! ow!

He got the kiss of death from the killer skull!

AND NOW IT IS MAY AND THERE HAVE BEEN MANY CHANGES. WHAT HAPPENED TO SHAGGY-BABA THE LUCKY CHIMNEY SWEEP WAS SHE BURNED HIM IN THE FIRE-PLACE. HE GOT TURNED INTO ASHES. AND HIS SMOKE WENT UP-UP-UP. I SHALL LEAP FROM BURNING BRIDGES. I GOT TIME. I GOT TIME.

GI-GI MAN

MY BEST FRIEND IS A GIRL, YOU KNOW HER, SPAZ-EYES GIGI, GIGI WITH THE MOVING SPAZMO EYES. GIGI WHO IS ALWAYS SAYING, "MAN, MAN, MAN." AFTER EVERY SENTENCE HER THING IS TO SAY, "MAN, HEY, MAN. I PLEDGE ALLEGI-GIANCE, MAN!"

AND MRS. TEACHER IS SO GREAT, MAN, OUR ASSIGNMENT, MAN, WAS TO DRAW OUR HERO, BABA, CAN YOU SHIBBY-SHA-BA-DIG-IT? I DREW THE SHAG-SHAG-SHAGGY-BABA AND GIGI, MAN, SHE SAYS "MAN! MAN! WHO IS THAT, MAN?" AND WHEN I SAY HIS WHOLE NAME, GIGI'S EYEBALLS GO FULL SPAZ. SHE FALLS DOWN.

MRS. TEACHER IS RUNNING TO US, GIGI HAS SPIT ON HER LIPS, AND HER ARMS AND LEGS ARE JERKING. MRS. TEACHER STAYS WITH HER AND THEN THE JERKING STOPS. THE NOT-FREDDIE IS STANDING THERE WATCHING. I AM SOMEWHERE ON THE CEILING.

BUT, MAN, IT WAS OK. MAN, IT WAS STORMS IN HER BRAIN, MAN, NORMAL, MAN, HER WAY, MAN. LATER, MAN, BEFORE THE DING-DONG-DING OF 3:00 AND YELLOW BUSES, MAN, SHE SAID "SKREDDY, MAN, THAT PICTURE, MAN, I NEED IT, MAN." SKREDDY WAS HER NAME FOR ME. SPAZ-EYES, SPAZ-EYES GIGI.

UNCHANGE

AFTER SHAGGY BABA WAS ASHES AND SMOKE, THERE CAME OLD BUDDY, MADE AT FIRST OF HAIR FROM MOM'S HAIRBRUSH THAT SHE PULLED FROM THE BRISTLES AND ROLLED IN A BALL AND SET IN THE ASHTRAY WITH THE CIGARETTE BUTTS.

AND THEN CAME THE SMELL AND THE SOUND OF HIM WHEN SHE STUBBED OUT HER BURNING CIG INTO HIS CENTER AND HE CRACKLED AND MADE SUCH TERRIBLE SMOKE. BURNING HAIR. BURNING HAIR. OLD BUDDY WAS ALIVE.

AND NOW IT IS MAY AND SHE STILL ISN'T TALKING. SHE SETS DOWN MY FOOD AND SHE FOLDS UP MY LAUNDRY. MAYBE I WILL MAKE HER SOMETHING VERY NICE FOR MOTHER'S DAY. MAYBE I WON'T.

IN THE FAIRY TALES READ BY MRS. TEACHER THERE ARE CRUEL STEPMOTHERS. THEY NEVER CHANGE TO NICE. THERE IS A LOT OF MAGIC POWER IN THE STORIES THAT CAN TURN ONE THING INTO ANOTHER, BUT I NEVER HEARD A STORY YET WHERE A CRUEL MOTHER BECOMES KIND.

HulaGirl

SKREDDY IS HER NAME FOR ME AND SHE TELLS ME SECRETLY, SECRETLY SHE IS MANY THINGS, SECRETLY SHE IS A BOY, AND SECRETLY— BUT THE PLAYGROUND MONITOR BLEW HER WHISTLE AT US AND YELLED.

GET YOUR BEHINDS <u>OUT</u> OF THOSE BUSHES, NOW!!!!

AFTER THAT, EVERYONE SAID, "OOOOH! YOU PLUS SPAZ-EYES, SPAZ-EYES PLUS YOU." SECRETLY SHE'S A BOY AND A FISH AND SUPER-STRETCH THE RUBBER MAN. AND I TOLD HER I WAS A DOG AND A GHOST AND THIS IS WHAT ME AND GIGI TALK ABOUT. NOT LOVE.

BIRDS LOVE SPAZ-EYES GIGI. THERE IS THIS ONE CROW THAT IS ALWAYS IN THE TREE BY OUR ROOM AND IT WATCHES HER. WHEN SHE GOES TO THE PENCIL SHARPENER, THE CROW HOPS DOWN THE BRANCH TO GET CLOSER.

WE HAD A TALENT SHOW, AN ALL-SCHOOL, AND SHE DID A HULA DANCE, MADE HER HANDS SAY OCEAN AND VOLCANO AND RAIN. THE PEOPLE WERE SNORT-LAUGHING, THE TEACHERS SAID, "SHH!" THEY SAID, "HUSH", THE MOON ROSE AND THE TRADE WINDS BLEW, AND THE STARS CAME OUT ONE BY ONE BY ONE.

TRANSFERS

SHE WASN'T COMING BACK. WE WOULDN'T EVEN HAVE A SINGLE DAY OF THE SUMMER TOGETHER EVEN IF WE COULD HAVE MANAGED IT. HER DAD WAS MILITARY, SHE SAID. HER DAD WAS SOME KIND OF ARMY.

IN THE LAST TWO WEEKS OF SCHOOL THE AIR ON THE PLAYFIELD WAS WARM AND GOOD TO BREATHE. WE PLAYED LONG KICK-BALL GAMES WHILE MRS. TEACHER CALLED EACH OF US ASIDE TO ASK US WHAT WE THOUGHT ABOUT. SITTING IN THE SHADE ON A FOLDING CHAIR.

MO-VING?

MOVING AWAY?

YEAH, MAN. THESIUS, MAN.

SHE SAID, "OF ALL THE THINGS THAT ARE ON YOUR MIND, WHAT IS ON YOUR MIND THE MOST?" IOWA, IS WHAT I ANSWERED. THESIUS, IOWA. THERE IS A SECRET ARMY BASE IN THESIUS AND THESIUS ISN'T ON ANY MAP. SPAZ-EYES GIGI WAS HAVING HER UP'S. THE BALL ROLLED TOWARD HER. SOMETIMES IT JUST IS NOT WORTH IT, MAKING FRIENDS.

SKREDDY, MAN! SKREDDY! HEY SKREDDY!

HEY, SKRED!! SPAZ-EYES!! SHE'S CALLIN' YA!! HEY!

MRS. TEACHER DIDN'T AGREE OR DISAGREE. HER STOMACH WAS STICKING OUT. SHE WAS GOING TO HAVE A BABY. SHE WASN'T COMING BACK EITHER. SPAZ-EYES GIGI KICKED A DOUBLE. FROM SECOND BASE SHE CALLED MY NAME JUMPING. DUST CLOUDS LIFTED AROUND HER FEET. SOMETIMES IT IS JUST NOT WORTH IT AT ALL.

HEY!

SKRED-DY! CHECK ME OUT, MAN!!

SKREDDY.

BURNING QUESTION

MARLYS WON A SPELLING PRIZE AND COULD GO TO A GIFTED CHILDREN'S SLEEP-AWAY CAMP FOR FREE, FOR THE SUMMER IF MOM WOULD JUST SIGN THE PAPERS. MOM SAID SHE WOULD THINK ABOUT IT.

PLEASE, PLEASE, PLEASE, PLEASE, PLEASE, PLEASE,

I SAID I'LL THINK ABOUT IT.

PLEASE, PLEASE, PLEASE, PLEASE, PLEASE.

THAT WOULD LEAVE ME WITH MAYBONNE BUT MAYBONNE RAN AWAY WITH JUST FIVE DAYS LEFT IN THE SCHOOL YEAR. "PLEASE, MAMA, PLEASE," SAID MARLYS. SHE HAD TO TURN THE PAPERS IN. THEY WERE ON THE KITCHEN TABLE WITH A PARKER PEN BESIDE THEM. "WHY WON'T YOU TALK TO ME?" ASKED UGLY OLD SPAZ-EYES.

MOM HUNG UP THE PHONE. FOR $300⁰⁰ MY AUNT SAID SHE WOULD TAKE ME AGAIN. FOR JUNE, JULY AND AUGUST. MY COUSIN ARNOLD'S HOUSE. MAYBE I COULD MOLLIFY HIM, SAID MY AUNT. "HA!" SAID MOM PICKING UP HER CIGARETTES. "NOW WHERE THE HELL ARE MY MATCHES? WHERE ARE THOSE DAMN PAPERS, MARLYS?"

PERMISSION FOR MY SON/DAUGHTER

MOLLIFY. MOLLIFY. SIRENS SCREAMED OUR WAY. THE NEXT-DOOR NEIGHBOR'S UGLY OLD GARAGE WAS ON FIRE, FLAMES SHOOTING UP OUT OF EXPLODED-OUT WINDOWS. "WHY?" SAID SPAZ-EYES GIGI, FOLLOWING ME ALL AROUND. "WHY WON'T YOU TALK TO ME?" I SOCKED HER HARD IN THE STOMACH. "THAT'S WHY," I SAID.

DEAR GIGI

I DID NOT KNOW YOU COULD DO SOMETHING TO A PERSON, AND THEN BEING FRIENDS WITH THEM WOULD END FOR ALL TIME.

GIGI.

GIGI.

GIGI.

"IT WAS JUST ONE SOCK IN THE STOMACH," I TOLD HER, "SOCK ME IN THE STOMACH, THEN, COME ON," I SAID. I FOLLOWED HER ALL MORNING RECESS AND THEN SHE WENT IN THE GIRLS' LAVATORY TO GET AWAY FROM ME.

GIGI.

GIRLS

AND IT WAS LIKE THIS FOR TWO MORE DAYS, AND THEN CAME THE LAST DAY OF SCHOOL. AND I TRIED TO GIVE HER A NOTE AND SHE KNOCKED IT OUT OF MY HANDS.

GIGI

WHAP!

AND I HAVE LEARNED FROM THIS. YOU DON'T SOCK A PERSON IN THE GUT WHEN THEY TELL YOU THEY ARE MOVING AWAY BECAUSE ALL THAT HAPPENS IS THEY GET ON THE YELLOW BUS AND YOU NEVER GET TO SAY GOOD-BYE, AND YOU NEVER SEE THEM AGAIN. OH. GIGI. GIGI.

SCHOOL

HELLO, FAG

"HELLO, FAG," SAID MY COUSIN ON THE TELEPHONE, "GUESS WHAT? YOU'RE NOT COMING. HERE'S MY MOM." AND THEN MY AUNT SAYING SHE DIDN'T NEED TO TALK TO ME. GET MOM.

OH.

OH.

I'M SO...

SAD.

WHO IS IT?

THERE WAS A LITTLE BIT OF SILENCE AND THEN A LOT OF SHOUTING AND THEN THE PHONE SLAMMING. THE NEWS WAS FANTASTIC BUT I COULDN'T SHOW IT. MOM WAS SO FREEZING MAD.

I TOLD HER I WAS OLD ENOUGH TO STAY HOME BY MYSELF, I REALLY WAS. AND AFTER MORE SCREAMING, SHE SAID OK, WHAT THE HELL, WHAT ELSE COULD BE DONE?

BECAUSE I HAVE TO WORK!

I HAVE TO!!

YES.

YES.

NOT LIKE I HAVE A CHOICE!

NO.

AND SO BEGAN MY SUMMER OF WANDERING TO PLACES I HAD NEVER BEEN. MOM WOULD LEAVE FOR WORK AND I WOULD COUNT TO 300, AND THEN, WITH MY HOUSE KEY AROUND MY NECK ON A SHOELACE, I WOULD STEP OUT INTO THE WORLD.

HEY, MAN.

WHAT IT IS!

BE FREE.

725th LETTER

DEAR GIGI, I KNOW YOU WILL NOT GET THIS LETTER, I AM NOT EVEN WRITING THIS LETTER, I AM JUST THINKING THIS LETTER TO YOU, THIS LETTER NUMBER 725.

THERE HAVE BEEN MANY PEOPLE WHO HAVE SOCKED ME IN THE STOMACH OF LIFE AND I NEVER STOPPED LIKING THEM. IT IS JULY. WHAT I AM DOING FOR A LIVING THIS SUMMER IS GOING AROUND. RIGHT NOW I AM AT THE ZOO.

THERE ARE PEACOCKS SCREAM-
ING AND MOMS SCREAMING
AND HOWLER MONKEYS GOING
INSANE. AND VERY MANY ANIMALS
THAT WILL NOT LOOK AT THE
PEOPLE, THAT KEEP THEIR BACK
TO THE PEOPLE, AND THE PEOPLE
SHOUT, "HEY! HEY YOU! HEY LAZY!"
THEY THROW THINGS.

GIGI, WHEN YOU QUIT LIKING
ME BECAUSE I SOCKED YOU
VERY MEANLY, I WAS VERY
SURPRISED. I DID NOT KNOW
IT WAS POSSIBLE OR EVEN
LEGAL TO QUIT LIKING A PER-
SON FOR THAT. I THINK IF
I WERE AN ANIMAL AT THIS ZOO
I WOULD NOT LIKE THE PEOPLE.
I WOULD NOT LIKE THE PEO-
PLE AT ALL AND I WOULD NOT
HESITATE TO EAT THEM.

YOUNG MAN

"FREDDIE," SAID MOM, "WHY ARE YOU TALKING LIKE THAT?" I SAID, "LIKE WHAT, GROOVY MAMA?" SHE SAID, "THAT'S MAYBONNE'S HAT YOU'RE WEARING." I SAID, "FREAK OR BE FREAKED, CAN YOU DIG IT? CAN IT DIG YOU?"

"FREDDIE," SAID MOM. "YOU SOUND IDIOTIC." I SAID, "DOWN WITH THE MAN. THE MAN IS A FAG. I AM ALSO A FAG. WE ARE ALL FAGS. BUT I AM EL FAGTASTICO!" THE MOTION OF THE SLAPPING HAND OF MOM WAS TOO SLOW! I, SKREDDY 57, EL FAGTASTICO NUMERO 57, WAS TOO FAST! "COME BACK HERE!" BUT SKREDDY 57 DID NOT OBEY!

I WILL NOT BE TAKEN ALIVE!

OR DEAD!

HE VANISHED! THEN HE WAS BEHIND CAROUSEL'S VARIETY STORE! <u>THE</u> <u>MAN</u> PUT THE STORE OUT OF BUSINESS! HE IS EVIL! THE BACK DUMPSTER WAS SO FULL! OLD THINGS THAT NEVER GOT SOLD FROM EVERY HOLIDAY AND HALLOWEEN ESPECIALLY! EL SKREDDY NUMERO 57 HAD AN EYE PATCH AND A CAPE! HE WAS FEELING VERY VERY GOOD!

HE HAD HIS MISSION IN LIFE! VIVA EL SKREDDY! VIVA EL SKREDDY! HE WAS STANDING IN THE DUMPSTER SHOUTING THIS WHEN HE NOTICED A DOG WATCHING HIM FROM BEHIND SOME WEEDS.

OH. HI.

FREE DOG

FREE DOG, JUST SITTING THERE FOR ANYONE TO TAKE. WHEN I SQUATTED DOWN TO SEE WHAT WAS THE MOOD OF THIS FREE DOG SITTING IN THE WEEDS, HE DIDN'T RUN. A YELLOW-COLOR DOG, OLD IN THE FACE.

I SAID, "HERE, BOY. HERE, MAN." THE FREE DOG STOOD SLOWLY. I STARED AT HIM. HE STARED BACK. FREE DOG.

"NO!" SCREAMED MOM. "OUT!" LOOK AT THAT THING! HE'S SICK! TAKE HIM BACK!"

"BUT MOM," I SAID, THERE IS NO BACK TO TAKE HIM TO." SHE SHOUTED, "OUT! NOW!"

I MADE A SIGN FOR THE CARS ON 23rd AVENUE: "FREE DOG!" HE LAY IN THE GRASS. THE CARS BLASTED PAST US. NO ONE STOPPED. HE WAITED WITH ME AND STOOD UP, AND I KNEW HOW HE FELT ABOUT EVERYTHING. ABOUT THE WORLD OF DEAD GRASS AND SCREAMING PEOPLE AND BEING ALONE AND THE CARS THAT JUST KEEP ON GOING. FREE DOG.

Free DOG.

HE LOOKED AT ME AND I LOOKED BACK AND THEN HE WALKED AWAY. I JUST STOOD THERE WATCHING HIM GET SMALLER AND SMALLER. FREE DOG, IF I WAS OLDER. FREE DOG, IF LIFE WAS DIFFERENT. FREE DOG, THIS BOOK IS FOR YOU. FREE DOG, FREE DOG, WHERE-EVER YOU ARE.